ANNA
KEEPS HER PROMISE

ANNA
KEEPS HER PROMISE

Translated by Joan Tate

ANNA KEEPS HER PROMISE

Martha Sandwall-Bergström

BLACKIE

First published as *Kulla-Gulla haller sitt lofte*

First published in Great Britain 1978 by Blackie

ISBN 0 216 90531 1

Blackie & Son Ltd
450 Edgware Road, London W2
Bishopbriggs, Glasgow G64 2NZ

Printed in Great Britain by
The Anchor Press Ltd
Tiptree, Essex

One

"Anna . . . Aaaaannnnaaaaa . . . Aannnnnnnnaa . . .!"

She could hear their calls from a long way away and in the gathering darkness could just see the children crowding out on to the porch to welcome her. She untied her head-scarf and waved it at them, giving herself a breather as she did so. You soon got out of breath on the hill, especially if you were already a little tired. Washday at the mansion had been hard work and then she had half-run all the way home in her anxiety. You never knew, leaving the children at home all day—things happened so easily, sticks falling off the hearth and perhaps starting a fire, for instance. But now she could see the cottage, dark and ramshackle, but in its place there on the brow of the hill, and she could breathe freely again. She waved her kerchief again before gathering up her fair hair and once again tying the cloth round her head. It was cold, and she felt the draught on the back of her neck. Her feet were wet and cold after the day in the washhouse and her skirts were wet, too, rustling stiffly round her legs in the cold. If she stood still for any length of time, she would surely freeze to the spot.

A figure on the porch broke away and came rushing down the hill to meet her. Some of the others may well have wished to do the same, but there was such a shortage of shoes good enough to go out in that they had to take turns, two pairs of clogs for four pairs of feet. From the sight of the single figure coming towards her, she realised that John, the eldest of the children, had not yet returned with the ox-cart from the day's charcoal-hauling. She sighed as she thought about it. John was so weak and delicate and the charcoal-hauling was a heavy job for an eleven-year-old; much worse than the day-work at the big house that Anna herself had done this week instead of Ellen, her mistress and the children's mother, who was still in hospital. So Anna could no longer help John with the charcoal.

"Anna . . . Anna . . ." The clogs came sliding down the icy slope, bringing Addie with them; Addie, who was five and the troublemaker in the house. It was not his turn to have the clogs, and as one of the youngest, he should have stayed indoors. He had simply taken them because it was fun skating down the hill. Anna was just about to reproach him for such thoughtlessness, when she suddenly saw that he was carrying his little sister on his dangerous ride. She managed to catch her just as the much too large clog slipped off Addie's foot and he sat down hard on his behind.

"Are you out of your mind, boy!" she cried, snatching the child up into her arms. The little girl was wearing nothing but a few worn rags and was wet, so Anna had to open her coat and surround her with her own body's warmth. With both arms round the child, she was unable to give Addie the slap he had earned. Anyhow, she had other things to think about, because the little body inside her coat was shaking with cold.

"She seems to be ill in some way," she said uneasily.

"She's been whining all day long," said Addie, holding on to Anna as he struggled up the bank. It was not easy going, either, as the clogs seemed to have a life of their own when it was slippery, especially if they were twice as big as the feet inside them.

"She just kept on and on whining," said Addie. "And when Vera tried to feed her, she said she didn't want it. So I ate it instead. And then Vera tried to heat the water for the gruel, but the pan tipped over and Vera burnt her arm, a big blister, and then the fire went out, and when Willie was cutting sticks to light it again, he cut his thumb with the knife . . . it bled awful, it did. So there was only me left to look after the baby and so I took the clogs," said Addie, justifying himself and grasping Anna's skirts as hard as he could to stop himself slipping backwards down the slope. "Don't go so fast, Anna. I can't keep up."

"We'll soon be there," said Anna, thinking about everything she had to do. Another work shift awaited her now. The cow, Skolla, was in the barn waiting to be milked. Straw had to be fetched for the ox when it was back from charcoal-hauling, because John would be exhausted and unable to help. Wood had to be brought in and water fetched. The six-year-old twins were supposed to do that, but the disasters of the day had no doubt put paid to it. And the fire had to be lit, the cottage heated and the children fed. Potato-porridge? Perhaps if she could nip a few from the cellar again. Karlberg had been angry when he had seen the potato store after gleaning. It was supposed to last the whole winter and leave enough over for seed in the spring. Perhaps they'd better stick to the usual cornflour, though it was bitter and musty and the porridge would be the same. But if they were hungry enough, no doubt it'd go down.

"But you'll have some sugar with it," she whispered down into her coat to the little girl, so that the greedy Addie should not hear. She had saved a lump of sugar, a big one, in her coat pocket. They had been offered coffee at the big house. The kitchen girls had come out with wonderful hot drinks in baskets to the washerwomen in the washhouse. Cream and a lump of sugar for each of them, and a thick soft slice of bread with syrup on it. Anna would have liked to have saved it for the children, but the syrup had made that impossible. She would hardly dare tell them how delicious it had been, as that would have made them even hungrier. But the sugar-lump remained untouched in her pocket for the little girl, and for her alone, because she needed it most. She had become so quiet and listless lately, no more bouncing noisily round the cottage, only whines and awkwardness. Her chubbiness had gone and her legs were so crooked she could no longer stand upright on them.

"When your mother comes home, things'll be all right again," she said, to console the children as well as herself. If only Ellen would be better soon and come home. "Because then you can stay at home all day with us," the children filled in. They had already forgotten what it was like to have their mother there. "When Mother comes home, she'll go out to work and you'll stay at home with us."

"No, the other way round," said Anna briskly, setting about the chores in the house. "The fittest must take on the hardest work. I'll probably have to go out to work all winter and I'll be happy if I can manage it."

Two

The next week, the work was the first of the Christmas preparations. A pig had been slaughtered and Anna joined the other women at cleaning out the intestines down by the river. The icy water chapped her fingers and her nose turned bluish-red, but it was the same for them all, so no use complaining.

In the afternoon, they were offered coffee again. They were invited into the warm manor kitchen, and after the day down there by the icy river-bank, it was like stepping into paradise. Anna had never seen anything so grand before as this kitchen, its walls covered with polished copper pans and light-coloured paint, a white cloth on the table. Respectfully, she sat with the others round the table, the delicious smell of hot coffee in her nostrils. They were offered real coffee, not the coffee brewed from peas and rye they had at home. And in front of each cup lay two wheat rolls, sweeter and whiter than they ever had at home, even at Christmas.

Anna bit cautiously into one of them, thinking that she had never tasted anything so delicious before. Slowly, little pieces at a time, she ate her way through half a roll, thinking about the children at home. In her thoughts, she cut the other roll into five pieces and gave them to them. But each piece was so small, and there she was, munching away at a whole roll all by herself. With a great effort, she took the half-eaten roll out of her mouth and together with the other untouched one, slid it into her dress pocket.

At that moment, an older woman came out into the kitchen and they all rose to their feet and curtseyed. The woman was wearing a blue dress with a white collar and had a starched crimped cap on her head. She was the landlord's housekeeper, Mademoiselle Modig, who had been in service for twenty years, and ever since the death of the landlord's wife had been regarded as the ruler of the house.

She gave them all a nod and a look, but suddenly stopped in the middle of the floor and stared at Anna.

Anna, who had just thrust her roll into her pocket, flushed.

"I was thinking about the children at home," she mumbled. "They like something nice sometimes, them too."

But Mademoiselle Modig went on staring at Anna and Anna grew more and more embarrassed. She brushed back her hair with her chapped fingers, tucking away the curls that had come out of her plait during work, and straightening out her cardigan at the throat, fastening a button.

But Mademoiselle Modig went on looking at her, until in the end Anna took the rolls out of her pocket and put them back on the table. Perhaps it was not allowed to take food home with you.

But then Mademoiselle Modig woke up.

"No, keep them, child," she said. "Keep them."

She looked at Anna again.

"I've not seen you before," she said. "What's your name and where do you come from?"

"My name's Anna," the girl answered shyly. "I'm doing Ellen Karlberg's stint, from Kulla. She's in hospital in town."

"Oh, yes, now I know," said Mademoiselle Modig. "But you're not Karlberg's daughter, are you?"

"No," said Anna, shrinking from having to repeat her story to yet another inquisitive crowd of listeners.

But Mademoiselle did not ask any more questions. She inspected the sausage skins that had been laid out on the draining-board, found them well rinsed and scraped, and then she left with a nod at the women.

A few days later, it was again time to go to the manor. The Christmas cleaning had to be done and it fully occupied three women from the crofts and two of the indoor servants. All the upholstered furniture was dragged out into the yard and beaten. Curtains, draperies and cloths were washed and starched, the pictures taken down and dusted. Anna spent all day on her hands and knees, scrubbing with a brush, soft-soap and sand. When it came to the drawing-room floor, Anna learnt something new. The floor was different from anything she had ever seen before. It had a smooth hard brown surface and was as shiny as a mirror, just as she had heard people say. It was called a parquet floor, one of the maids told her, when she was showing Anna how to clean it.

Anna crawled and polished with a woollen cloth and wax to make the shiny floor even shinier. Now and again, she looked up and respectfully stared at everything else in the drawing-room, the fine gilt furniture with its silk covers, the Chinese porcelain urns and ornaments of silver and ivory. There were pictures on the wall, too, and the biggest and most beautiful of them hung above the sofa and chairs grouped along the long wall.

It was a portrait in oils of a fair-haired girl, leaning against the arm of a sofa and looking out with friendly serious eyes. They looked so alive that every time Anna looked up from polishing the floor, the girl seemed to be standing there looking at her.

In the end, Anna got up and tiptoed over to the picture, and the closer she got the more alive the girl seemed. She seemed to want to nod at Anna as she stood there leaning slightly forward, looking down into the room with her serious eyes, dark-blue, slanting a trifle towards her temples in a remarkably strange way.

The girl was wearing a silk dress with puff sleeves and draperies on the skirt fastened with rosettes of the same silk. Round her waist was a tight blue belt with glittering stones set in it. Her hair curled down towards her shoulders in fair ringlets, but it didn't look at all untidy, Anna thought, but quite neat, although it wasn't plaited.

There was a little gilt plate with something written on it on the frame of the picture. Anna crept a little closer to see what it said.

Annemaria Beatrice Frederika Sylvester, at the age of twelve . . .

Anna blinked in astonishment, closed her eyes and looked again. Yes, that was right. It was her name there . . .!

A wild joy leapt up her. This must be the landlord's beautiful daughter, the one they said had run away abroad and was perhaps dead, as nothing had ever been heard of her since. It must be her, must be. And she, this beautiful noble little lady had exactly the same names as Anna—the same awful old names that made everyone laugh.

Anna was so pleased that tears came into her eyes. It was like a reward for all the insults she had suffered because of her unusual old-fashioned names. She couldn't help smiling as she stood there.

"Just think," she whispered, looking up at the portrait.

"Just imagine . . . we've got the same names, you and me . . . just imagine that." Her smile widened, her whole face radiant. It was a long time since she had felt so marvellously happy.

She stayed there for several minutes, smiling at the girl in the picture, feeling good inside, just as if she had met a dear friend or someone she belonged to—as it must feel to have someone to belong to. And the girl in the picture looked down at her in such a friendly way, almost with understanding and complicity in her eyes.

One of the maids came in and saw Anna standing there in front of the picture, a young girl with a hard face and malicious eyes, who liked bullying her companions when Mademoiselle wasn't looking. She grabbed Anna's plait and led her back to work.

"Don't think you can stand idling about like that," she snapped. "That's not what you're here for. And what you don't get around to doing, some other poor devil's got to do, so get a move on."

Anna got obediently down on her knees and began polishing away with all her might to make up for those neglected minutes. But she was smiling to herself all the time and now and again she looked up and nodded at the girl gazing down at her from the picture.

"Just think," she kept saying to herself. "Exactly the same names . . . it's as if we belonged, you and me."

Three

When she got back home that evening, she told John, and he was almost as pleased as she was. He brushed his red fringe aside and looked at her with glowing eyes.

"You know what," he said. "Next time they're silly and laugh at you at school, we'll tell them about that."

"Yes, let's," said Anna, smiling at the effect it would have on Linnea and the others.

She had brought back a roll with her this time, too, and the children were gathered hungrily round her. They were all pale and sallow, and even Addie's cheeks had begun to fall in. Karlberg complained every day that too much food was being eaten. Every time he took a few hours off from charcoal-burning to see how things were at home, he worried even more. They hadn't even got to Christmas yet, but there was hardly anything left but seed-potatoes in the cellar, and the rye-flour was also almost at an end.

"You're a bad housekeeper," he scolded Anna. "You've no hand with food. You must see to it that the children don't eat so much."

It was the same out in the barn. The hay up in the loft was almost at an end and the straw-stack outside was beginning to look like an old hen losing her feathers. But the ox had to have fodder as long as the heavy charcoal-hauling went on, so it was Skolla who went without. That meant their milk supply suffered. Skolla gave no more than a couple of litres now, and that didn't go far. So the porridge and gruel were mostly cooked in water.

The children grew pale and sallow-cheeked, hungry for food like small starved dogs. The twins fought over scraps if Anna was not near to keep them in order, and while they fought, hitting and pulling at each other, Addie nipped in and stole whatever they were fighting over.

But the youngest one, before so keen on her food, was quite different. She wouldn't eat at all, but just turned her head away whimpering from the gruel. Her legs were crooked, her head large, her skin puffy, and she hardly ever laughed.

"Here you are, little one, little one," said Anna, going over to the cradle with the babe's share of the roll. "Here you are, try this now. Manna from heaven, it is. Just you look."

She stopped and then rushed over to pick the child up in her arms. The little face was blue and the small limbs knotted in cramp.

"Oh, heaven help me," cried Anna. "She'll die. She's choking. Help me, dear Lord, help me."

She put the child down on to the table and tried to force open her mouth with a spoon she had snatched up.

Afterwards, when the convulsion was over and the child lay gasping and relaxing in her arms, Anna wept aloud.

"I can't go on leaving you here in this way," she said, looking at the children silently crowding round her. "You're as pale as death, the lot of you, and blue round your eyes. Perhaps you bigger ones will manage until there's more food. But baby here, she's too weak. She'll go if things don't change in some way. And I promised Ellen that you'd be well looked after."

"Wise Manda . . ." John began, because she was the first person everyone thought of when help was needed for a sick person.

"Her medicines won't help any longer," sighed Anna, shaking her head. "Wise Manda's done her best." Wise Manda had given the babe ointment as well as her special patent medicines for rickets; ash from four kinds of wood, burnt one Thursday when the moon was on the wane, and mixed with a little sugar to make it appetising.

But nothing helped, they could see that. Her illness grew worse and Anna knew that it was a dangerous stage when the child had convulsions.

Next morning, after she had done the chores, she wrapped the babe in a sheepskin, put on her kerchief and coat, told John to keep the children in order, and then set off out into the bitter cold. She plodded through the drifts towards the forest, glad that Karlberg was not at home to stop her.

Dally-Peter was standing on the steps when she arrived. Everyone was rather frightened of him as he was considered to be in league with the underworld. He looked like a little grey hobgoblin in all that white snow, his beard almost down to his knees.

But Anna was not afraid of him. He had looked after the babe when she had strayed away in the forest in the autumn, and he had been kind to her.

"Good morning," she said, breathlessly. "Here I am, come to see you at last. You've had to wait a long time for us to come, haven't you?"

She stood still for a moment, waiting for Dally-Peter to invite her in, but when he said nothing, she bravely moved a little closer.

"You see, the babe's ill. I think she's near to death, and no medicine or anything helps. Wise Manda has done her best. Now I've come to ask you . . . if you can cure her?"

The old man looked at her for a long time.

"People have at one time or another come to me to ask me to put their pains right," he said, in his lilting monotonous voice. "And evil deeds and black magic, that I'm supposed to know about. But no one's ever come with such a wee mite before. No, no, girl, the art of healing's not my line of country. No, no, you'd better go back."

"But, please," said Anna. "It's the babe you found in the forest. You might at least say something to her, if nothing else."

She held the bundle out to him. "She's cold," she said. "Please let us in, sir."

It was as dark as night inside the cottage, as the little window was covered with a blanket against the cold. Otherwise it was warm in there, a few logs burning on the hearth. The goat lay ruminating in one corner, and the three small pearl-grey hens had companionably settled on its back. Beside the hearth sat the black cat, purring by its dish of milk. It got up when Anna came in, stretched itself comfortably and rubbed up against her legs.

"Please, look at her, sir," pleaded Anna. "She's sick. She doesn't even take any notice of your beard."

She loosened the sheepskin round the little body, and showed him the crooked limbs and large head.

"She's got the rickets, and Manda's medicines do no good."

The old man said nothing, but stood looking at the child. Then he took her into his arms and began to sing. But the babe didn't move, just smiled a tired little smile that at once vanished again. The old man scratched his head under the grey hood.

"Can you help us?" said Anna, hoping that in some way he would make the babe well by magic.

The old man went on scratching his head for a while. Then he picked up a cup from the table and went over and gave the goat a shove. It got up obediently with the three little grey hens still on its back, and the old man bent down and began to milk it. He went on until the cup was full of strong yellow goat's milk, and then gave it to the babe to drink. At first she turned her head away, as she always did when food was offered to her nowadays, but then she seemed to change her mind and began to drink, emptying the cup and stretching out her hands for more.

"Not today," said the old man. "Tomorrow. That's strong food for a stomach not used to it. She'll get better," he went on. "You can go home now, girl, and rest assured."

"Thank you," said Anna, getting up, confused by the simplicity of his magic. Drinking goat's milk from a cup; would you believe it?

When she left, the old man went with her, just like the last time. But he had the goat on a rope and one of the little grey hens under his arm as they plodded through the snow.

When Kulla came into sight, he stopped and gave her the end of the rope to which the goat was tethered.

"One cup of milk a day for the first three days," he said. "Then she can drink as much as she likes."

Then he took the grey hen and thrust it under Anna's free arm.

"She must eat the eggs it lays as they are. Don't boil them or fry them. And while the snow still lies, boil up some pine-needles and give it to her to drink. And when the snow goes and spring comes, take the first young green you see and boil it for her. That's life, that is, girl."

Anna squeezed the cackling hen under her arm and stared.

"Do you mean . . . the goat . . . and the hen? But we can't take them. We can't take your goat and hen from you."

"They must live in the kitchen," said the old man. "They're used to that, and I'll bring fodder for the goat this afternoon."

With that he was gone, swallowed up by the forest, and Anna could do nothing else but make her way home with goat, hen and child.

At home there was uproar among the children, but the goat and the hen soon settled down. The goat at once chose a corner in the alcove by the open fire, and contentedly cackling, the hen settled down on its back. Then it was only a matter of what Karlberg would say when he came home.

When Anna stepped out on to the porch that evening, there was a large heap of sweet-smelling meadow-hay and a bundle of dried leafy branches lying on the snow, and she realised Dally-Peter had been there with fodder for his animals.

Karlberg did not come back from the forest until almost a week later. Then he had finished at the charcoal stacks and the last one had been dismantled. The remaining loads would not be taken down to the estate until after Christmas, so there was a brief pause in the work. To celebrate, Karlberg had been down to see his friend the miller, where he had had a few drinks he reckoned he deserved, with all the trouble he had with his wife in hospital and the children half-starving at home.

The children were deathly quiet when he came in that evening, and Anna, smelling the drink at once, was filled with anxiety.

Karlberg wove his way unsteadily across the floor, in passing spitting a stream of snuff into the fire, then sinking down on to the sofa. The light was dim in the room, but the babe in her cradle kicked her legs and chuckled.

"She's better, then?" said Karlberg, raising his head a little.

"Yes," said Anna.

"That's good," said Karlberg, getting up again to spit in the fire. The stream of snuff fell this time to one side—Karlberg wasn't so careful when he was drunk—and hit the goat on the nose as it lay ruminating in its corner in the dark. The goat snorted and shook itself. The hen on its back had just fallen asleep with its head under its wing, and now let out a terrified cackle.

Karlberg glared incredulously into the darkness of the corner, thinking he was seeing things.

"What . . . what the . . .? What's that lying there in the corner? What in heaven's name is it . . .?"

"It's Dally-Peter's goat and hen," Anna began anxiously. "You see, he . . ."

"*What* did you say?" shouted Karlberg. "Dally-Peter's goat?"

"Yes, you see . . ."

"Dally-Peter!" cried Karlberg. "What's that evil old hobgoblin got to do with us, eh? What've you been up to, girl? What've you been doing?"

"I took the baby to Dally-Peter," said Anna frankly. "And he's given us his goat and a hen . . . She's to have the milk and eggs, he said . . . and you can already see how much good it's doing her."

But Karlberg wasn't listening to her. "In league with that old rogue again, are you?" he raged at her. "What you mean, running off into the forest like that, stupid girl?"

He boxed Anna's ears so that she fell against the wall, dropping a plate she had had in her hand. Then he rushed at the goat in the corner.

"Out with you, evil critter!" he roared. "Out of my house, evil goat, you."

He grabbed the goat's horns and tried to drag it out of the alcove. With a terrified cackle the hen flew up straight into Karlberg's face. He tumbled backwards, letting go the goat, which now joined in and went into the attack. The children over in the corner screamed as if their lives were at stake.

"Father! Father . . . Father! . . . Let us keep the goat! Father, please, Father . . .!"

The first butt struck Karlberg at the back of his knees, and as he was already unsteady on his feet, he lost his balance and fell forward. The next butt hit him a bit higher up and was so hard they heard the bang.

Karlberg bawled and yelled. He tried to get up several times, but each time the goat butted him again. In the end, it decided enough was enough, turned right round and with its head up, returned to its corner. The hen had been sitting up on the chest clucking with terror all the time, but now spread its wings and flapped down on to the goat's back. Karlberg got up carefully, shook himself, lay down on the sofa and fell asleep.

When he woke the next morning, Anna had already milked the goat and was feeding the babe. She was drinking the luke-warm milk with obvious delight. Karlberg sat on the edge of the sofa, regarding Anna and the children in silence. When he left the room, he glared angrily at the goat and the goat glared angrily back, but there was no more fighting. Karlberg was as a rule fairly good-natured, and only turned violent and forgot himself when he had had too much to drink.

Four

On Christmas Eve, Karlberg went to town to see Ellen. He had about fourteen miles to walk and started in the early hours while it was still pitch dark outside. Anna made porridge for him, and he ate a big enough helping to last him all day. He said he was going to stay the night at a farm near town and would not be back until the following morning.

So Anna and the children were alone at home for Christmas, and they were pleased. They had rice and cinnamon that Ellen had saved from the Christmas before, when food had been more plentiful, and they also had milk to make it with. Milk was more plentiful now the goat had come to the house and was giving extra rations.

In the evening, the rice bubbling on the stove and the children gathered round to breathe in the delicious smell of cinnamon, the goat suddenly grew restless and pattered bleating across to the kitchen door.

"She wants to go out," said John, looking doubtfully at Anna. At this time of the day, in the Christmas dark, it was inadvisable to go out or even open the door. Because during the night now, the dead were wandering the roads in their shrouds, and hobgoblins and gnomes were scuttling across the hard snow, squealing and grumbling between the houses, all heading for the light and warmth of the living. But if you opened the door, both good and evil might come in, so it was best not to. Anna and John had been down to the barn before it had grown dark to give Skolla and the ox a little extra fodder and wish them a happy Christmas. They didn't want to open the door again that night.

But the goat stayed by the door and kept on bleating. The wind whistled and whined outside and fresh snow rustled over the icy crust, as if someone were padding about and sighing outside.

"There's someone out there," whispered the twins, their teeth chattering. Anna and John looked at each other, the same thought in their minds—Greatgran. Perhaps she had walked the long road from the churchyard, driven by a yearning for her earthly home and human warmth and light?

Anna resolutely grasped the door-handle, unlatched the door and opened up. An icy blast swept in a cloud of snow, making Anna jerk backwards. But the goat let out a delighted bleat and leapt straight out into the night.

"Oh, help, now she's run away!" cried Anna, running straight out after the animal, regardless of ghosts. "Fia . . . Fia . . . come back, oh, please come back!"

But Fia had not run away. She was standing on the corner of the house rubbing herself against a little old man in a pointed hat.

"Oh . . ." said Anna with relief. "It's you . . . come in, do . . . come inside in the warmth, and welcome welcome . . ."

She held the door open and curtseyed. "Please come in, come in."

The goat the children had named Fia came in first and behind it came Dally-Peter, looking round cautiously.

"Karlberg's not at home," said Anna. "And we're just going to have our Christmas rice. Come in, come in. No one should be out longer than necessary on Christmas Eve."

The old man stepped inside, blinking against the light like an old owl, lumps of ice hanging from his beard just like on the ox's tail. The twins put their heads together and giggled.

"Children," said Anna, looking sternly at them. "Come and say hullo properly, all of you. That's it."

She pulled up a chair for the old man at the best place by the fire, and laid another place on the table. Then there was a miaow outside, and when John opened the door slightly, Dally-Peter's black cat squeezed its way in through the crack.

"Prrr," it said, rubbing itself against the children's legs. It was thin, its sides gaunt, visible signs that it was missing the nourishing goat's milk.

Before they all sat down at the table, Anna went to fetch the baby to show Dally-Peter that she was already on the mend. She was plumper and her eyes were brighter, and when she saw Dally-Peter's beard, she stretched out and grabbed a handful of hairs.

Dally-Peter cackled with laughter, the children squealed with delight and Anna's eyes filled with tears. This sign that the baby was on her way back to normal was the best Christmas present she could have wished for.

When they had eaten, she took out the bible to read the Christmas gospel. She was used to hearing it on Christmas Eve both at the orphanage where she had spent her early years, and at Hermansson's. But when she opened the bible and was about to start, she suddenly felt anxious. If Dally-Peter really was a troll as people said . . . trolls couldn't withstand the word of God. Either they were destroyed or turned to stone, and she didn't want any harm to come to the baby's benefactor.

Carefully, she began to read, a word at a time, glancing sideways so that at the slightest sign, she could stop.

But he just sat there, quiet and expectant on his chair, and in the firelight his eyes shone far down in the tangled grey whiskers. Like the children, he tried to clasp his hands together in prayer. It looked clumsy and strange when the hairy claw-like fingers pressed against each other. The twins stared in fascination at him, the troll, in league with Satan, sitting there at their table with his animal paws worshipfully clasped in prayer.

". . . and at that moment the Angel of the Lord appeared and a great multitude of the Heavenly Host," Anna read, "and they promised the Lord and said . . ."

She stopped for a moment and listened. They could hear steps outside. There was a fumbling and scratching at the door.

"Honour to the Lord on High," Anna read, trying to put strength into the words, so that whoever was fumbling at their door would depart, if it was one of the evil ones. "Honour to the Lord on High and . . ."

The door opened and Karlberg came in. His leather jacket and cap were covered with snow, his face ruddy from the wind and cold, as well as something else. He smelt of drink.

He pulled off his cap, staggered unsteadily forward, stopped and glared at Dally-Peter.

"What the . . ."

Anna rose slowly, the bible still in her hand, her back very straight, and she seemed to grow taller as she stood there, her eyes turned towards Karlberg serious and clear, glowing in the firelight.

"... Peace on Earth and Goodwill," she said in a high clear voice. "Peace on Earth and Goodwill to all men ..."

"Hrrm," said Karlberg. "Hmmm ... what?"

"Peace on Earth," said Anna, still standing between him and Dally-Peter, now pressing anxiously against his chair. "It's Christmas Eve and Peace on Earth, Karlberg."

"Mmm ... perhaps it is," said Karlberg, scratching the back of his ear. He stood swaying back and forth, as if thinking. He could see the made-up beds through the doorway and he was tired after his long walk; perhaps he would prefer resting to fighting. He walked unsteadily across the floor towards the bedroom and Anna followed him, keeping herself like a buffer between him and Dally-Peter. Still fully dressed, he flung himself down on one of the beds and Anna carefully closed the door on him.

A long time later, when the younger children had been put to bed and Dally-Peter had quietly padded out into the night, John was still seated at the table with his chin in his hands, staring into the fading embers on the hearth.

"Anna," he said, looking across at her where she was busy at the sink. "This Christmas Eve ... I'll never forget it. Like a peal of bells from far away, it was. Like the scent of flowers in the gardens of Paradise ... or something, Anna. It was good to have been through."

Anna nodded without replying. John often talked about his paradise and sometimes she grew tired of it. She thought she had grown so much older while she had been here at Kulla, and she was beginning to know the difference between sagas and reality. But as long as John believed in his paradise and dreamt about it, that was good for him and she did not grudge him that. She thought about Dally-Peter far up there in the darkness of the forest, and about Greatgran in her solitude in the churchyard and about Ellen—how things were with her now—and she felt melancholy. She was tired and would have liked to cry.

But John was smiling with such pleasure over there at the table, she couldn't spoil his happiness.

Five

It was a hard winter for all the crofters in the district. The beasts lay weak with hunger in the barns, no longer able to stand on their feet, and the children were gaunt-eyed and pale. But at Kulla they managed, and although Karlberg said not a word about it, he knew it was thanks to Dally-Peter. The goat gave plenty of milk, the nourishing milk that kept the children plump. And the little pearl-grey hen laid an egg a day for the baby. And each week, a heap of sweet-smelling meadow-hay and dried branches lay outside the barn door. The goat did not eat it all, as both Skolla and the ox had a share, and that was what saved them.

But Ellen stayed on in hospital. Karlberg sighed, feeling sorry for himself, and more and more often went to see his friend the miller for consolation.

Anna struggled bravely to keep her promise to her sick mistress. She became part of the family, big sister and mother to them. She worked hard day in and day out, fixing things and thinking for them all on the croft, in so far as her twelve years allowed her.

The responsibility gave her dignity and authority, and Karlberg less often took to blows and abusive words to her. Even when he came home drunk and noisy, he held her in respect, and Anna soon learnt that the less frightened she was and the calmer she was, the easier it was to manage his outbursts of rage. But if things went wrong, she quickly left the cottage with all the children, the goat and the hen, and they spent the night in a heap of straw in the barn. The children all relied on her. They had forgotten she was not one of them and saw in her support and help and protection against all that was bad and difficult and troublesome. They loved her as much as their own mother, yes, perhaps even more. She was never irritable and cross and never hit them, neither slaps nor blows with the broom or the fire-iron. When she came home in the evenings from her day-work, they all crowded into the doorway to welcome her with their joys, their troubles and the funny nicknames they had made up.

"Oh, there you are, Annie-pannie . . . we've been waiting and *waiting*, 'cos the fire just *won't* burn up, Anna-danna-manna . . . baby's wet again and there aren't any dry drawers, Annie-minnie-minnie. And we're so *hungry* . . . and we're *cold* . . . and we've been waiting and *waiting* for *so* long for you, Annie-pannie-danna-manna-minnie-minnie . . ."

Anna comforted them and helped them, and worked and toiled, and when her soul wearied of all the tasks, she comforted herself by thinking that all would be well when Ellen came home. Because although Ellen was not always a pleasant companion, at least the responsibility of the children would then be lifted from Anna's shoulders.

John started school again, but not Anna. Karlberg had been down to Mr Bromander and asked for her to be excused until Ellen came back home. "One has to have some use out of the girl now we need her," he said to Mr Bromander, and the school governors understood him.

Anna did the two days a week work at the manor instead of

Ellen. It was mostly indoor work, so fortunately not too heavy for a half-grown girl. Anna liked it at the big house, and when she came back from there, she always had some titbit for the children. Because she always carried out her work in an orderly and industrious manner, she soon won favour with Mademoiselle Modig, and the stern housekeeper often gave her a friendly nod or a pat on the head as she went on her inspection round.

Whenever Anna had a chance to look at the picture in the big drawing-room, she felt especially happy. Annemaria Beatrice Frederika Sylvester always looked down at her from the picture in such a friendly way, a kind of glow in the depths of those serious eyes. Sometimes she seemed to nod at Anna.

"I know you," she seemed to want to say. "I know you, Anna, and I'm your friend. We must be friends, as we've got exactly the same names."

One cold spring day, when the sun was warm and the snow-drifts had started melting, Mademoiselle Modig commanded Anna to go with her up to the attics to air the clothes that were hanging there or were packed away in chests.

"You must remember," she said to Anna. "This is the time of the year when the moths set to work and one has to take care of one's possessions . . . the woollen clothes must be taken out into the sun and be brushed and shaken."

"Yes," said Anna, storing away the words in her memory, although at home on the croft, the only clothes they had were those in use.

She unpacked chest after chest of camphor-smelling shawls, rugs and walking-out clothes. There were clothes of all kinds there, and as Ellen had said, enough to go round all the poor children in the parish.

"This is Her Grace's clothes-chest," said Mademoiselle Modig, clasping her plump hands as if over a monument. "And in these two we still keep the little mistress's dresses, the ones she wore as a child."

They lifted the lid and unpacked the clothes, hung them up in the sun and brushed them thoroughly. Among them was an old-fashioned dress of stiff white silk and Anna let out a little cry when she saw it. It was the same dress as on the portrait.

"Oh, dear, dear. Oh, dear," sighed Mademoiselle Modig, running her hand down the draperies of the skirt. "She was such a pretty little girl, and remarkably good, too. Everyone said so. Though she had a temper, too, that she did . . . there were heated tussles between her will and her father's more than once . . . yes, yes, oh dear, those were the days, those were."

Mademoiselle stroked the rustling silk, sunk deep in her thoughts, and Anna longed to hear more.

"I heard it said that she went away . . . that she ran away," she tried cautiously, in an attempt to awaken Mademoiselle from her memories.

"Yes, yes," said Mademoiselle. "Yes, she did. Young people are so foolish when they're in love. She was twenty when it happened. Met a painter . . . he was a nothing and I never even saw him, because the Patron wouldn't allow the little mistress to bring him home. Then the Patron wanted to marry her off to a fine gentleman well suited to her, a nobleman, and a wealthy one, too, and he tried to arrange the marriage at once, because she was so gone on that painter-fellow. Well, it was probably mostly Her Grace behind it all, egging him on, though how should I know? But it was wrong, anyhow, to treat her like that—almost by force so to speak. She at once turned stubborn and stiff-necked. They couldn't break her. And then one day she was gone."

"Didn't she ever come back?" said Anna, listening intently. It was like hearing about a friend. Everything that the little girl on the picture down there had experienced seemed to be very much her concern.

"No, she never came back," sighed Mademoiselle, rocking to and fro, her hands clasped. "She went abroad with that wretched painter. He had one of those scholarships to travel around on. Artists don't live like ordinary decent folk. They don't seem to have any roots. But it was hard to understand how the little mistress could cause her parents such grief. But as I said, when young people fall in love, you just can't rely on them any more, and the Patron should have understood that. He'd been young himself, too, once upon a time. But you forget, you forget . . ."

"Didn't you ever hear from her . . . in any way?" said Anna, her voice trembling slightly, afraid Mademoiselle might change the subject or just stop talking.

"She wrote once," said Mademoiselle, her eyes on the white silk dress as if talking to it and not to Anna. "The letter was to me, and was supposed to be a kind of secret, I suppose. She wrote that she was well and happy, and she asked after her parents, and whether they had got over the worst by then. They had travelled round several countries, she wrote, and she had a little daughter. Just think, the little mistress a mother. Yes, I cried when I read that, that I did. I'd always been so fond of her. I wrote back. The address was a post-office in southern Germany, and I asked her to come back again, because they were grieving for her here, and would be sure to forgive her and resign themselves to what had happened—I wrote that. And then another letter came that said that she and her painter and the little child were coming home in the spring. But they never did. They never came at all."

"But, perhaps they will?" said Anna naively.

"No, they won't," sighed Mademoiselle, shaking her head. "It'll be twelve years soon since that letter came. And her little child, who was six months old then, according to the letter, would be a big girl now. Yes, about like you, if they're still alive at all. But they aren't. They've surely gone."

Mademoiselle suddenly fell silent when she heard someone calling for her from below. It was the landlord's voice and she hurried down the steep stairs.

"Brush all the clothes properly," she called back to Anna. "And don't forget to put clean paper in the chest before you pack them in again. I'm trusting you to do it properly now, girl. I haven't time to stay up here with you any more. Oh, how the time flies! It'll soon be dinner-time. Yes, yes, Mr Sylvester, I'm coming."

Anna was left alone up there. The sun shone through the attic window and the flies that had survived the winter woke and buzzed against the panes. Anna brushed all the clothes, but her gaze kept going back to the white silk dress on its hanger, gently swinging back and forth in the breeze. It was so like the portrait down below, the same draperies on the skirt and the same finely worked rosettes holding them, the same glittering blue stones on the waist band.

Now and again she ran her fingers down the silk and listened to the light rustle, then she took the dress off its hanger and held it in front of her . . . they were the same size, she and her namesake downstairs.

A great yearning like a fever rose in Anna. She wanted to feel the dress on her, feel what it was like to wear such rustling material and what it was like to be a girl of the gentry.

She listened breathlessly down the stairs but could hear nothing, so she swiftly put the dress over her head, pulled it down over her thick homespun dress, buttoned it up with trembling fingers and drew the belt round her waist.

The dress was a little tight on her in places . . . she must be a little larger than the girl down there after all. Perhaps that came from work, she thought. A girl from the gentry had no muscles or strength in her sinews.

She smiled a little and took a few tentative steps in the long skirt, hearing the material rustling and billowing out round her. How fine and light it was . . .

She swung round experimentally . . . wondering if the little mistress had run round the rooms in her father's house and laughed and swung her skirt . . . like this and like that . . .

Anna danced on the rough boards of the attic in her leather-soled socks. Never before had she done any dance steps . . . it was the dress, the fine gown that had done it. She swung back and forth, enjoying the way the old-fashioned skirt billowed and swayed round her. She pulled the ribbon off her plait and shook out her hair. Her cheeks glowed and her eyes shone. She had forgotten Anna from Kulla, the servant girl from the orphanage. Now she was the Annemaria Beatrice Frederika on the picture down below.

Mademoiselle Modig came back a few minutes later to send Anna on an errand to the village store. The landlord was having gentlemen guests and they had no spices for the punch. Mademoiselle trudged heavily up the attic stairs, thrust her head over the top and was just about to call out to the girl above.

But her lips, just forming the word Anna, froze halfway, cutting the word off. Instead she let out a long "Loooordie", her cheeks turning as white as the pleated cap on her head. There was a sound like sacks of flour falling down the stairs and then silence.

Anna stopped dancing and hurriedly came back to earth when she saw Mademoiselle's starched cap appear above the top of the stair. Without knowing where to go or what to do next, she stayed standing in the middle of the attic floor in her silk dress, scarlet in the face as she met Mademoiselle's gaze. Then she rushed to the top of the stairs and saw Mademoiselle lying in a faint below.

But the next moment Mademoiselle came to and rushed up, calling loudly for the landlord.

"Mr Sylvester, Mr Sylvester! Quick, come up to the attic, Mr Sylvester!"

Beside herself with fright, Anna tugged at the dress to get it off. But her trembling fingers could not undo the awkward hooks and buttons. For a moment she fought between the choice of throwing herself over the balcony or hiding behind the clothes closet, but then she came to her senses and chose to stand up straight and answer for what she had done.

She was standing there in the middle of the floor when the landlord came up, her back very straight and her hands no longer trembling. She lifted her chin a trifle defiantly, but her eyes were calm and clear. Her loosened hair curled round her head in untidy fair ringlets.

Mr Sylvester had snatched up his riding crop when he had heard Mademoiselle's cry and rushed upstairs in the belief that there were thieves or intruders in the attic. He was panting a little, for he was old and not used to leaping up steep stairs.

He held the riding crop high and Anna waited for him to strike her, as he had done that day in the potato field. But his arm fell to his side and his forehead paled below the grey hair-line. He took a step back, fumbling for support.

"My God!" he whispered, staring.

Then Mademoiselle's head again appeared above the stairs,

her starched cap awry and strands of hair escaping from her neat coiffure. Her face was blotchy with agitation.

"I thought I was seeing ghosts, sir," she gasped. "But the girl is real and alive and the likeness must mean something."

"Auto-suggestion," said Mr Sylvester, but he was still white in the face and the hand holding the crop was not very steady.

"I recognize you now," he went on. "You're the girl I spoke to on the potato field. You're the daughter of one of my crofters . . ."

"Not a daughter," Mademoiselle whispered. "She's only in service at Karlberg's. She's an orphanage child."

"Oh, is that so?" said the Patron without interest. "Well, what's your name again, girl?"

Anna's lips moved. She was frightened and found it hard to get the words out.

"Annemaria . . . Beatrice . . . Frederika," she said.

The landlord stared and Mademoiselle gaped. She had never heard any other name except Anna.

"That's not possible," snapped Mr Sylvester, suddenly agitated again. "You're lying."

"No," said Anna firmly, and as she had learnt at Karlberg's, she grew calmer as the others grew more agitated. "Those are my names, sir, and that was why I wanted to try on the dress . . . because it was *hers*, and because we had the same names. But I promise I'll never do it again, sir," she added, suddenly ashamed and regretful. "I . . . I don't know what came over me."

The landlord drew a deep breath to calm himself.

"Come on down to my office and we can talk about it," he said.

Five

Downstairs, Anna was told to sit on a chair in front of Mr Sylvester's great oak desk, and he asked her a great many questions. She had to tell him all about her life, about the orphanage, the shipwreck, which she didn't remember at all, but had heard others tell about it, and the little gown with the names embroidered on it, the names they had given her again at her baptism to be sure.

Mr Sylvester wrote notes about everything into a book, watching her attentively all the time. Anna was confused and did not understand the point of it all. But when Mademoiselle helped her off with the tight silk dress and she was allowed to go, the landlord took her hand in his.

"Maybe we'll be seeing rather more of each other," he said, his voice thick and peculiar, then he turned swiftly away, and Anna left in a state of confusion.

But Mademoiselle Modig, whose worst agitation was now over, pressed a list of spices and some coins into her hand.

"Run on down to the store in the village now, and fetch these," she said. "There's no point in putting ideas into your head before we're sure."

Anna thrust her feet into her clogs, wound a kerchief round her head and set off, more confused than ever.

"They can't think I'm the landlord's lost daughter, can they?" she thought to herself, as she trudged through the slush. But then she laughed loudly at her own stupidity. The idea was ridiculous. Miss Sylvester had been grown up and married to a painter and had a child and . . .

Anna stopped and stood absolutely still, a great joy welling up inside her, so tempestuous that it took her breath away.

". . . and the child would be a big girl now," Mademoiselle had said. "It's nearly twelve years since I had that letter and the child was six months old then . . ."

"I'm twelve and a half," whispered Anna, pressing her hands against her thumping heart. "Yes . . . yes . . . yes . . .! I feel it . . . that's it . . . I knew we belonged together, you on that picture and me. Dear Lord in Heaven, help me so that I don't die of happiness."

She sank down onto a snowdrift at the side of the road, overwhelmed by her thoughts and emotions. That *was* it. She knew it. She had a father and a mother . . . not alive, true, but she *had* them all the same. And she knew what her mother looked like, what kind of clothes she had worn and how she had behaved to people round her. She had roots and origins, like everyone else.

She stayed there on the roadside until the snow began to melt and felt wet beneath her. Then she jumped up, remembering her errand. But she didn't run any more. She danced along on her way.

She had got halfway to the village when she was suddenly jolted out of the dream world she had been in and brought back to earth again. She heard a sound that was only too familiar. It was John crying, a whimpering, plaintive, frightened weeping.

Her dance came to an abrupt end. She immediately forgot

Annemaria Beatrice Frederika and remembered only that she was Anna from Kulla and that John was crying round the corner.

She glanced quickly up at the sun. Yes, this was the time John came back from school, presumably in the company of Karl as usual.

Anna started running and soon caught sight of them round the corner. The ditch along the road was full of melted snow and Karl was in the process of ducking John into it. He was holding him by the back of the neck with his great broad hands and laughing at the helplessly struggling John.

"Scared, are you? Scared of a dip, scared of being baptised, John the Baptist, eh? Then here's a lesson to you, you . . . You'll catch fire, with hair as red as that!"

"Please let go," John was pleading, shaking all over. He had already been ducked twice and his red hair lay in wet strands down his pale blue cheeks, his thin legs in white knitted stockings kicking and struggling against the slushy snow.

"Your name's John, isn't it, eh?" shouted Karl, laughing. "Then you oughtn't to mind being baptised, John the Baptist. Don't kick me like that, or I'll chop your head off and put it on a dish."

John was the first to see Anna, when he twisted his head round out of fear of being ducked again.

"Anna!" he cried out. "Anna, Anna!"

Karl quickly turned round at the shout and saw Anna running towards them, the slush splashing out from her clogs. He still had that clog of hers fresh in his memory since the last time, and so thought it advisable to escape while he had a head-start. He flung John away and set off down the road.

"Anna," said John, his teeth chattering as he got up on all fours in the slush. "Oh, Anna."

"Hurry on home and get dry!" she shouted, running on after Karl.

She increased her speed a little and calculated the distance between the two of them. She wanted to catch up with him about a hundred yards further on, where there was a ditch as deep as the one here, but Karl was running at a wild gallop, and she was afraid he would pass it before she caught up with him.

Slowly she began to catch up on him. Karl was panting and gasping so loudly that she could hear him. His body was fat and ungainly from being given too much food at home, and he turned round so often he soon lost a lot of his headstart.

"Yes, go on panting and puffing, you," she thought. "Lollop along like an escaped loony, if you think that'll help you. I'll catch you, you mark my words. I'll catch you."

Then Karl turned round again. The girl was after him again, and the distance between them had grown smaller. He could see the slush splashing like steady rain behind her feet.

He clenched his fists and rushed on as fast as he could, scared by her calm methodical pace. Anna's skirt was flapping like a sail, her hair curling damply on her forehead from sweat. But she was still breathing calmly, without apparent effort.

Karl was skittering and galloping along and seemed to him to be getting nowhere. His mouth was open, and he was breathing heavily, his arms and legs flailing, and he kept turning round to look.

At the next corner, he gave up and turned round to face her, his face scarlet with effort.

"What do you want of me?" he panted, stretching out his clenched fists and standing with his feet apart.

Anna's even pace neither increased nor slowed down. She

ran straight on, as if to run past him, her face calm, without anger. Karl stared, not understanding her intention, and relaxed for a moment.

Then she was on him. She leapt on to his back like a tiger clawing at its prey. Her hard sinewy arms clamped round his neck, a jerk, another . . . and big fat Karl fell back flat on his back in the slush. He yelled loudly and struck out at her, wildly and furiously, like the lion in the fable being attacked by a wasp.

"I didn't mean no harm! To John. I didn't mean no harm," he shouted.

"I don't mean any harm, either," said Anna, rubbing a handful of muddy snow into his face. "I just mean that you're now so filthy you need a bit of a wash . . . Oh, you look dreadful," she added, rubbing another handful into his face.

She strained against the road, slipped, kicked off her clogs and thrust her feet down again. Then she rolled Karl right round. He watched whichever way she went, and fought back as best he could. But he was lying badly, and he was afraid of another dose of slush. He was losing strength from shouting, too, and his fine leather shoes could find no grip in the mud. With a bellow and a splash, he rolled down into the ditch.

Anna stood looking down and watched him come up again.

"What are you bellowing about?" she said. "Can't you take a bath? What . . . can't you?"

Then she retreated a short distance away and shouted at him to hurry on home to his mother and get some dry clothes on.

"You're as wet as a babe in arms," she shouted rudely, watching him trudging off homewards, crestfallen and dripping wet. "And learn once and for all that the biggest isn't always the strongest . . . no, indeed."

But when she was standing there wiping down her clothes that had got dirty from the mud from the road, her fighting spirit faded, and she felt sad and downhearted.

"I don't understand all that much," she mumbled. "But at least I know there'll never be any peace if things go on in this way."

Seven

When she got back to Kulla that evening, John was sitting shivering and shaking on the sofa, so cold that his teeth were chattering. It was cold in the cottage, as the fire had gone out. Anna ran out to fetch wood and lit the fire and boiled some milk and cinnamon for him, before she started on anything else.

"Drink it up while it's hot," she told him. "You look quite blue, as if you were sickening for a chill."

John drank the hot drink and felt better. His hair was still wet from his ducking in the ditch, and Anna rubbed him carefully with a sack cloth to get him dry. Meanwhile she told him what had happened at the manor during the day. The children gathered wide-eyed round her.

"If that's true," said John, "then the landlord's your grandfather . . . just think, you could say Grandfather to him."

"Silly," said Anna, laughing. "I couldn't ever do that."

"And everything the landlord owns would be yours one day," said John. "All the estate and forests and fields and farms and *everything*, Anna. 'Cos he's got no one to leave it to. And you could go dressed in fine clothes with a parasol over your head, and ride in a fine carriage drawn by the bays."

"And people would curtsey to you right and left and on all

sides," cried the twins with delight, and Anna laughed loudly at such a foolish thought. Her laughter was infectious and soon they were all falling about each other with merriment. Addie hadn't understood much of what it was all about, but he laughed too, just for the sake of laughing, and then the baby was gripped by the general merriment. She hauled herself up from the floor against the sofa and began bouncing up and down.

"Hoo-hoo-hee."

When they took no notice of her, she grew jealous and tried to attract their attention. She took a few tentative steps on her legs, that were now beginning to look chubby and straight again, then stood for a moment trying to keep her balance, then she carried straight on across the floor.

The twins were the first to see her. They stopped laughing and just stared.

"Look, look, look at her!" they shouted. "Look . . . she's walking!"

From that moment onwards, the baby walked, and when Karlberg came back a little later, his eyes widened in surprise.

"Well, who'd have believed it!" he said.

"We must write and tell Ellen," said Anna. "And we must get her baptised soon, too, Karlberg." She had remembered about that during her spot of bother with Karl.

Karlberg scratched the back of his ear.

"Hmm, yes," he said. "She's not baptised, is she? Though . . . we can't go to the minister with a brat that can walk. How would that look?"

"But we can't let her spend the rest of her life a heathen," said Anna.

"You can't baptise a brat that can already walk," Karlberg

repeated, embarrassed at the thought of what the minister would say.

The next morning, John complained of a headache and stayed in bed. His face was bright red and his body burning hot, although he maintained he was so cold he couldn't stop shaking. Anna boiled some more hot milk for him and wrapped him up in the best sheepskin they possessed. She heated some water and gave him a hot footbath, because she knew that drew the heat from his head and would ease the pain.

"What a fuss over the boy!" said Karlberg crossly. "Just leave him be. He'll be all right tomorrow. He's got to be, come what may. The last of the charcoal's got to be got down to the yard. The surface won't take no sled soon, so it can't be left no longer."

John lay shaking under the sheepskin all day, but when Karlberg told him sharply to get up for the charcoal hauling the next morning, he obeyed.

"Headache," said Karlberg. "That's not nothing. It'll pass, when you're out in the fresh air."

He accompanied John and the ox up to the stacks and loaded up, but then John had to manage on his own, as a message had come from the manor house that Anna should come, although it wasn't one of her days.

"Those gentry, they doesn't stop to think for a moment," muttered Karlberg. "Just sending messages for the girl on a day like this. They just thinks a crofter sits with his hands in his lap all day, doing nothing, week in week out . . ."

Anna was not given any work to do at the house that day. She was taken to the landlord in his office again, and the maidservants she passed in the kitchen stared at her as if they'd never seen her before.

In the office sat Mr Sylvester and an unknown gentleman, who looked very learned and asked Anna much the same questions as Mr Sylvester had the day before. And like Mr Sylvester, he wrote notes down in a book, and finally took her with him into the drawing-room and stood her beside the picture. After having looked at her for a while, he said that the "likeness was fantastic".

"It's not a matter of two ordinary faces," he said to the landlord. "Your daughter on the picture has character in her features with that unusually fine oval face and those remarkable eyes . . . and then the names. It can't just be chance."

Mr Sylvester turned roughly away and gazed out of the window.

"I want to be quite sure," he said briefly.

The stranger bowed. "I'll do my best, sir," he said courteously. "But the chances of finding absolutely definite evidence are very small or non-existent in this case. But as I said, I'll do my best."

Then they left the room, forgetting Anna, who took the opportunity of nodding and smiling at the picture.

"They can hardly believe it," she whispered. "But *we* know, don't we, you and me?"

Then Mademoiselle Modig came and took Anna with her into the little pantry where Mademoiselle took all her meals, separate from the servants. There was a tray with coffee and buns and little biscuits, and Anna was invited to sit down and have some. Mademoiselle Modig sat with her all the time, looking as dignified as if she were in church.

"Eat up, child, eat up . . . you're much too thin."

"The children back home are even thinner," said Anna,

hoping Mademoiselle would understand and let her take home the leftover buns.

But Mademoiselle's thoughts were elsewhere and in the end Anna had to ask her directly.

"I wonder if I might take a little home to the children," she said shyly. "It's not easy sitting here eating, while they're starving back there."

Then Mademoiselle woke up, went to fetch a bag and put all the food left on the plate into it.

Then Anna got up and thanked her, brushing the crumbs from her dress and waiting for Mademoiselle to set her to work. But Mademoiselle patted her head with her plump hand and said that she could go home for the time being. She needn't come for day-work for a while, the landlord had said, and Karlberg would be personally informed of this.

"When the time comes, we'll let you know," said Mademoiselle Modig. "Go now, my child. We'll see what the future brings."

Anna thanked her, curtseyed and left with a sense of loss. She had liked her day-work at the manor house, anyhow as long as it was indoor work. She had always been given good coffee and the rolls had always been enough for titbits for the children. And she would miss Annemaria Beatrice Frederika on the picture.

Eight

John was away a long time that day and Anna kept darting uneasily between the windows, looking down the hill. Karlberg came in for his evening meal muttering angrily "that the boy wasn't no good", as he could never do a job on his own.

"At his age I was as good as any other labourer," he boasted. "So he don't take after me, anyways."

"The best of John lies in his heart," said Anna. "He'll be a good man."

At that moment the ox could be heard bellowing down by the barn, and she drew a sign of relief. John was back now, anyhow. She put the pan back on the fire to heat up the porridge for him and blew on the embers until they flared.

"Funny way that critter's lowing," muttered Karlberg, helping himself to some more porridge.

Anna pushed her feet into her clogs and went out. In the dim light down by the barn, the ox was standing lowing outside the closed door. From inside, Skolla was answering him.

"John?" called Anna, looking round for some sign of him.

When she got down there, she found him lying at the bottom of the sled, as still as if he were dead.

"John . . . what's the matter, John?" cried Anna.

She clambered into the sled and lifted him up.

"John . . . John . . .!" she cried, shaking him. Then he came to and groaned weakly.

"Am . . . am I home now?" he whispered. "It took so long . . . it was so hard . . . today . . ."

Anna unharnessed the ox and pushed it into the barn, then helped John up to the house.

She got him on to the bed and pulled off his shoes and stockings. His feet were icy cold and she hurried to fill a hot-water bottle. Karlberg sighed over by the table.

"That boy is nowt but a trouble and nuisance."

"The road's long and hard," mumbled John. "But if you yearn hard enough, you'll get there in the end . . . am I there now, Anna?"

"You're at home John," said Anna. "And now you're to eat up your porridge and rest and . . ."

"I was so cold," whispered John. "And I had earache. I thought I'd never get there . . . but when things were at their worst, I heard them . . . the bells . . ."

"Stop talking nonsense, John, dear . . . just lie still and I'll make some nice hot tea for you."

She covered him with a sheepskin and tucked him up firmly.

"We shouldn't have sent him off like that, sick that he is," she said to Karlberg. "I promised Ellen the children would be all right while she was away."

"That don't mean we've got to keep coddling the wretched boy," muttered Karlberg crossly, glowering over in John's direction.

John stayed in bed and seemed to grow worse each day. Occasionally he was delirious and raved about strange things, but when he was conscious he complained of bad pains in his head and ears. Wise Manda came and poured homemade liniment into his ears and bandaged his head with ointments to "draw out" the pain. Sometimes the pain was so severe that he couldn't lie still, but sat rocking to and fro, his hands to his head, as if trying to stop it bursting.

He was tormented by the snufflings of all the others sleeping in the room at night and when Karlberg snored, it seemed to him as if glowing chains were being dragged through his aching head. In the end, Anna took him out into the kitchen at nights, so that she could care for him better, giving him water when he was thirsty and holding his hand when the pain was too much for him.

One night, she woke when he called to her, and slowly and laboriously she dragged herself out of the waves of sleep imprisoning her limbs and mind. She clambered out of bed.

"Yes, John . . . do you want some water . . . or what's the matter?"

He turned his eyes towards her, his head an aching boil that he could no longer turn on the pillow, his face thin and hollow beneath the long red hair, his cheeks scarlet with fever.

"I'll soon be there," he whispered. "Can you hear them, Anna . . . the bells . . . those silver bells."

"No, I can't hear anything . . . it's the fever, John, ringing in your head."

She took a cup of water and held it against his dry cracked lips, but he made no effort to drink. His eyes were looking at something beyond her, and she turned quickly round.

"What are you looking at, John?" she whispered. There was nothing behind her except the kitchen wall.

"A little further . . . only a few steps, Anna . . . the trees are in blossom and so are the flowers . . . the scent . . . it's coming in on the wind. I'm so close now . . . I'll soon be there."

Anna stared at him as she stood there shivering in her short shift. She was used to him raving, but this time it was something more than delirium, and his face had an alien and unfathomable expression. At that moment he looked like Greatgran when she had lain in the ox cart, her features smooth and untroubled. Anna fell to her knees and grasped his hands.

"No, no!" she cried. "You mustn't . . . don't go, John. Stay . . . stay with us, John, *John, listen to me* . . ."

He tried to free his hands. "Let me go, Anna . . . let me go . . . only a few more steps . . . they're waiting for me, those beautiful children in the meadows . . ."

"No, no, no, you mustn't . . . I promised Ellen . . . listen to me, John, dear sweet John, dear Lord in Heaven, let him stay with us . . . I'll do everything I can . . . I'll do everything you want me to. Just let him stay . . . I'll keep holding on, John, I won't let you go . . . are you listening, I won't let you go . . ."

"Let me go," whimpered John. "They're singing . . . and the bells are ringing."

But she hurled herself over him as if his small emaciated body was what she wished to hold back. She wept and prayed, promised and beseeched.

"John, stay, stay . . . John, dear heart . . . dear Lord, be merciful. What shall I tell Ellen if he dies? No, dear kind Lord, you must keep him with us here on earth."

She fought with death as she had recently fought with Karl, fighting him off, striking and retreating, weeping and beseeching, while Karlberg went on sleeping heavily in the bedroom, snoring like an angry growling dog.

"Let me go there," John pleaded. "Let me go, Anna . . . they'll close the gates for me."

"No, no, no!" cried Anna again. "I'll not let you go . . . I'm keeping you here, John."

As the morning light trickled in through the little kitchen window, Anna got up from the cold floor, her knees stiff and her legs blue with cold. She looked down at John. He lay sleeping against the straw pillow, but he was breathing more evenly and the feverish patches on his cheeks had faded. The corners of his mouth were turned down as if he were about to weep and his thin face bore an expression of boundless sorrow and disappointment.

Anna stayed looking down at him for a long time, then padded back to her cold bed, burying her head in the pillow and crying so that her shoulders shook. And she herself did not know whether she was weeping out of relief or regret.

Nine

After the crisis, John grew better. The pains in his head lessened and one day thick yellow matter began to run out of his ears. Wise Manda looked in now and again when she was in their direction and seemed satisfied with the course of events. "It's drawing out, the badness," she said.

But John himself lay there silent and weary on his straw mattress, a withdrawn look on his face. Anna hushed the children, trying to keep them quiet during the day, so that John would have rest and peace, but John did not seem to mind the noise any more, sometimes not even answering if anyone spoke to him.

"Time that there sickness was done with now," said Karlberg one day. "Just lying there, enjoying being coddled and spoilt, like some prince or other. Soon you'll have to get up and be some use, I'm telling you."

John was leaning back in his bed, looking in his school books, and did not reply. He didn't even look up.

"D'you hear what I says?" said Karlberg sharply. "This can't go on no longer."

When John still took no notice, he grew angry, and striding across to the bed, gave John a clip over the ear.

"Can't you even answer when your father speaks to you!" he shouted.

John whimpered and clasped his hands over his head, his eyes astonished and confused.

"What's the matter, Father? Why did you hit me?"

"Answer when you're spoken to!" said Karlberg. John looked at him, leaning forward a little and frowning.

"I can't hear what you're saying, Father."

"What the . . .?" shouted Karlberg. "Have you gone deaf, boy!"

John put his hand behind his ear and looked miserable.

"What?" he said.

Karlberg stood staring stupidly at his son for a moment, then went and sat down heavily on the sofa.

"So that's it," he said slowly to himself. "That, too. Nothing but trouble and nuisance, that's all he's been, wretched boy. And now to cap all, he's been and gone deaf."

One early spring Sunday, when the sun was warm, Karlberg scratched his head thoughtfully, then said to Anna:

"I met the new minister yesterday, and had a word with him about the little'un. We can go down and get it done today after evensong, he said."

"Oh, yes," said Anna, realising at once that he was talking about the baby's baptism. "Why couldn't you have said something about it before?"

"That weren't necessary," said Karlberg.

Anna pursed her lips. No, of course that hadn't been necessary, no indeed. Men had no idea about things. What would she put on the babe now in such a hurry, with nothing but rags in the house?

But they set off all the same and if the babe did not look exactly elegant in one of Addie's cast-offs and hand knitted socks, then the minister would have to excuse them. She was whole and clean, anyhow.

Karlberg carried her on his arm, for although she was good at walking, they couldn't let her try out of doors because she had no shoes.

It was a fine day and the sun warmed them. The snow had almost gone, and everywhere on the farms along the road, emaciated cattle had been let out to graze the heather and undergrowth.

Karlberg walked ahead with the baby, who was waving her hands and cooing with delight at the sun and all the new things she was seeing. Behind them came Anna in the black Sunday coat she had been given by her previous mistress. It was so old now that it was quite green at the seams. She had leather boots on her feet, but they were difficult to walk in because they were too small and pinched her toes.

Just before they came to the village, where the road led down to the mill, Karlberg stopped and handed the baby over to Anna.

"You got to manage on your own now," he said. "I haven't no time to do no more."

"But . . . but . . ." said Anna.

"The minister said he'd be waiting in the sacristy," said Karlberg, wishing to escape the embarrassment of his large unbaptised child. "Off with you, now, so you're not late." And with that, he turned his back on them and with long strides vanished down towards the mill.

The churchgoers were just leaving when Anna shyly went in with the child in her arms. The minister was standing in the sacristy in his black cassock, talking to a gentleman, and when

Anna had calmed down a little, she noticed it was the landlord. She curtseyed low, twice for the minister, as he was a man of God, and once for the landlord, whose superiority was only of the world.

"Please will you baptise baby," she said shyly in a low voice, holding out the child. Frightened by the silence and the dim light, the baby grabbed at Anna's plait.

The minister smiled kindly. "What's she to be called?" he said.

Anna was startled and flushed scarlet. The names . . . heavens, they'd forgotten all about them!

"Karlberg . . . he forgot to tell me," she mumbled.

"That's a pity," said the minister. "Haven't you even discussed names for her?"

"No," said Anna, ashamed. They were so used to calling her "baby" that no one had thought about names. They had simply been eager to save her from heathendom.

The minister thought for a moment. "If I remember rightly," he said. "An old woman related to Karlberg died last autumn. What was her name?"

"That was Greatgran," said Anna. "And her names were Sofia Katrina."

"Then it would be appropriate to call this child after her in her memory," said the minister.

Anna flushed again. Those awful, old-fashioned names. She felt sorry for the baby, as she knew just what that meant. But she dared not object to his suggestion, so said nothing.

"Beautiful, proud names," said the minister, taking the baby into his arms. "I hope she will bear them with honour."

The churchwarden came in and they lit two candles. Then they placed them and a silver bowl of water on the table. The baby was christened Sofia Katrina in the name of the Father, the Son and the Holy Ghost. She was quiet all the time, but when it was over she bit the minister's cheek.

When Anna came out again with Sofia Katrina in her arms, the landlord's carriage was waiting outside.

"We're going the same way," he said. "You can ride with me, my child."

The coachman jumped down from the box and held open the door for her and the baby, and Anna got in beside the landlord. The churchgoers standing talking outside stared at them, for never before had they seen Mr Sylvester allowing such poor people to ride beside him in his carriage.

They drove past group after group of churchgoers on the way, and everyone saw Anna sitting beside Mr Sylvester. In one of the groups, Linnea was walking with her parents, and Anna saw her mouth fall open in surprise.

"Yes, indeed," thought Anna, unable to suppress her pride. "Perhaps it is a sin, but it feels good. Yes, indeed, just you keep on looking."

The landlord sat in silence, looking at the girl beside him. Then he put his hand on her head.

"What would you think about coming to live with me at the manor—and being my little girl and growing up into a grand little lady?"

"I think it'd be like going to heaven," said Anna, her voice trembling a little. "But it's out of the question at the moment. I've promised to look after the children until Ellen comes back."

Mr Sylvester told the coachman to drive as near to Kulla as the road would allow, and when Anna got out, he again patted her on the head and said they were sure to be meeting again soon. He was expecting some letters and information on a matter that was important to them both.

"But I think I can say that whatever happens as a result of

my investigations, then I'd like to take you on," he said. "You can get ready to move down to my house later on."

Anna looked at him, her face radiant, her heart thumping. Then she took his hand and curtseyed both to him and the coachman in thanks for the ride, and set off on foot up the last slope.

Two weeks went by without any message coming from the landlord. Everyday problems piled on to Anna and she hadn't much time for dreams and wondering. But when things seemed most difficult and the work seemed heaviest, she could straighten up, breathe deeply and think:

"One day it'll all be over. And then I won't be Kulla-Anna any more. I'll be Annemaria . . . Beatrice Frederika Sylvester, and live like a princess."

One day the big house carriage was seen struggling up the hill and Mademoiselle Modig stepped out of it and came panting up the last bit.

"Mr Sylvester has sent me here to arrange for your move down to the manor," she told Anna, after greeting them and looking round the cottage. "He hasn't yet received evidence that you are what we think, it's true, but he's taken an interest in you nevertheless and wants to look after you."

Anna ran her hands down her apron in embarrassment, looking down at the children's heads crowded round her and peeping out at the stranger from the shelter of her skirts.

"You see," she said. "I can't leave until Ellen's back."

"That can easily be arranged," said Mademoiselle Modig. "Karlberg can get a housekeeper in the meantime."

"No, I'm afraid he can't," said Anna, smiling at the housekeeper's simplicity. "A housekeeper costs money and crofters haven't got any. And anyhow, I wouldn't feel easy about the children. You never know if a stranger would be nice to them.

And you wouldn't know if she'd be able to cope with Karlberg when he comes home drunk. Perhaps she'd just go, leaving the children alone with him."

"If that's so," said Mademoiselle. "Then things can be arranged another way. The children can be found other homes in the parish for the time being . . ."

"On the parish!" cried Anna in horror. "No, Mademoiselle, please don't say that."

"But you're on the parish yourself, child . . ." Mademoiselle began.

"Yes, that's why," said Anna.

She bent down and put her arms round the group of children clinging and pushing round her.

"They're so small and helpless," she said. "And John, the eldest, is deaf now, and can't manage among strangers. I don't want any harm to come to the children, I really don't, Mademoiselle. And I've given Ellen my word of honour. I'm responsible and can't leave the children until she's back home again." She straightened up and looked into the other woman's eyes.

"Then I can," she went on. "When Ellen comes home, then I'm free. I'll come then, Mademoiselle. My regards to Mr Sylvester and thank him most respectfully. Tell him I'll come as soon as I'm released from my promise."

Mademoiselle looked at her, clasping her hands across her stomach with a sigh and saying no more. But Anna stood watching the carriage rolling down the hill for a long time.

They were all waiting for a message from the hospital to say that Ellen could come home. Karlberg had walked the long way into town again, as he had begun to wonder whether the hospital was simply having him on. She had been there for so long and still hadn't recovered.

"I'll come and take her away some day," he said to the doctor. "She can lie abed at home." But the doctor had calmed him down. They had tried to cure Ellen's ulcers with diet and rest, but that had not succeeded. Now she was to have an operation. If it was successful, it was hoped she would soon be allowed home. The doctor promised to send a message via the manor telephone. All Karlberg had to do was to wait.

And back there at home, they waited, Anna and the children. The smaller children had almost forgotten Ellen, and Addie remembered only how she used to chase after him with the fire-iron. But Anna talked so often about her in such glowing terms that they began to yearn for her. If there was anything difficult or troublesome, Anna comforted them with the words:

"It'll be better when your mother comes back."

It became a kind of talisman. Everything would be better "when Mother came back". The food would go further and the children would have enough to eat, their fear of drunken evenings would fade, the spring would come with its warmth, and there would be no more troubles the day their mother came back.

"On that day things'll be better for all of us," said Anna.

The children thought and mused and wondered.

"When's she coming, then?"

"Soon," said Anna. "And when that day comes, we'll all show how pleased we are and you children can run down and meet her and call to her . . ."

"Welcome home! Welcome home!" cried one of the twins, imagining the scene.

Anna nodded. "That's right," she said.

Only John, sitting over by the stove whittling at an axe-handle, said nothing, as he could not follow what was being said. They had to speak right into his ear if he was to catch the words. But when he saw them laughing and joking, he came over, wanting to join in.

"We're talking about when your mother comes back," Anna explained into his ear, putting her arm round his shoulders. "It'll be good for the children to have her back again."

John smiled bleakly, as if the prospect was not entirely joyful.

"We'll lose you that day, Anna," he said slowly.

But Anna laughed, happy at the thought of the new life ahead of her.

"Silly," she said, lightly.

Ten

Anna was down by the barn chopping spruce for fodder for Skolla and the ox, all they had to keep them alive now the loft was scraped bare of every straw and no green had yet begun to sprout between the patches of snow on the ground.

As she stood there, Addie came running down from the house.

"Annie-minnie-minnie!" he cried. "Addie been so good, so good . . . all afternoon. And if they says anything else, they's lying, they is, 'cos I've been good."

He stopped and looked at Anna, his head innocently on one side. He had a bump on his forehead and cuts on his fingers. Anna stopped chopping and looked hard at him.

"Tell me at once what you've done, Addie."

"Only sat on the sofa singing, Anna. Only sung lovely about God and the angels all afternoon."

"Tell me what you've done," said Anna relentlessly. "What've you done to your forehead?"

"There?" Addie felt the bump as if in surprise. "That's where the clock falled down and hit Addie on the head."

"The clock?" whispered Anna. "Did it break, child?"

Addie avoided her gaze, listening in the direction of the barn.

"Lot of noise they make when they want food, them critters," he said.

"Did the clock break, child? How many bits? Tell me, quickly?" Anna's voice was shaking with anxiety. Ellen had a little tube of porcelain-glue on one of the shelves. Perhaps she could . . .

"About a thousand, I think," said Addie cheerfully. "They went all over the room. Under the sofa and on the hearth . . ."

"Heavens!" Anna dropped the axe and set off up to the cottage. The clock shaped like a church had become Karlberg's pride and joy and he had found some old works that he had managed to mount inside the porcelain shell.

"It's a blooming miracle, that's what it is," he used to say.

There was a terrible atmosphere in the house. The twins had crept quite quietly into a corner and John was sniffing and snivelling over a pile of porcelain splinters and a few buckled parts, tiny little pieces and slivers . . . a thousand bits, just as Addie had said.

"Heaven help us!" said Anna, feeling the floor sway beneath her. "It's Saturday and all, too, and Karlberg's perhaps been to see the miller."

"It was Addie," said the twins. "He climbed up on the sofa and then up there . . . we were in the kitchen and John was sitting with his back to him so didn't hear him."

"Was only going to creep into the church and sing a bit," sniffed Addie, he too now infected by fear. "And clock fell down all by itself . . . *all by itself, Anna.*"

"Father's coming, Father's coming!" shrieked the twins from over by the window.

Anna swallowed.

"Remember," she said sternly. "Not one of you is to say a thing. Not one, do you hear? Leave this to me. Do you hear?"

"Yes," they all said at once.

Karlberg came heavily trudging in and sat down at the table. Anna put out some bread and poured out the coffee, hoping to gain a little time. People were better-tempered on a full stomach than on an empty one.

"Here you are," said Anna, cutting an extra thick slice of bread.

But the twins could not bear the tension. Suddenly they lost their senses and both began talking at once.

"It was Addie, Father. It was Addie, on his own, Father. It wasn't us what broke the clock."

Karlberg looked over the top of his cup. "What? What did you say . . . the clock?"

"It was Addie what broke it," the twins shouted.

Karlberg's gaze went to the clock on the chest, found it missing, slid round the room . . . then he let out a bellow.

"The clock . . . my fine clock!"

"It was Addie!" the twins shouted again, bent on saving their own skins.

Karlberg let out another bellow and leapt to his feet so that the cups on the table tipped over. Addie screamed and hid behind Anna, who spread out her arms in front of him like a hen protecting her chicks.

"Karlberg, Karlberg, please, Karlberg," she cried. "We're sorry about what's happened. But please forgive us, please! It's done and can't be changed."

"Get out of my way!" shouted Karlberg. "Let me get at the boy."

"Anna, Anna, help me!" screamed Addie, clutching Anna's skirt.

"Father, Father!" cried John. "Leave him be, Father. Forgive him . . ."

Then suddenly a trap stopped outside the porch steps, and there was a knock on the door, a short commanding knock, and the landlord stepped inside.

"I've brought a message from the hospital, Karlberg," he said.

Silence fell in the cottage, all eyes on the upright commanding figure. Karlberg felt simple, as if God the Father himself was standing there in front of him in his poor cottage. He began fawning and scraping.

"You shouldn't have taken the trouble to come yourself, sir. I didn't mean you to go to all that trouble yourself, sir . . ."

"Karlberg," said Mr Sylvester solemnly. "Karlberg, my man, the message is such that I wanted to bring it myself. Your wife was operated on yesterday, but she did not survive."

"What?" said Karlberg.

He looked at the landlord, wide-eyed like a child who understood nothing. "What . . . what did you say, sir? She didn't survive . . . is . . . *is Ellen dead* . . . my Ellen . . ."

The last word rose to a scream. "My Ellen . . . *dead*?"

"Karlberg, my man," said Mr Sylvester.

"It ain't possible," said Karlberg. He sank down on the sofa and stared straight ahead of him, then suddenly covered his face with his great calloused hands and burst into tears.

The children stared at him in terror. Father was crying. They had never seen that before, nor could they even imagine such a thing possible. The sight was so strange and disturbing that if possible it frightened them more than the sight of his rage.

Mr Sylvester looked at Anna. She was still standing in the middle of the floor in her patched outgrown skirt and her leather-soled socks, her face small and thin and touching. She was also looking at Karlberg, wide-eyed and solemn, all round her the signs of need and poverty. Poverty lay in the rough boards of the floor, in the shabby furniture, in every corner of the cottage. Poverty shone accusingly from the pale faces of the children and round Anna's own lean, worn little figure.

The landlord, a commanding, cultured and wealthy man, sensed the accusation and was uneasy. A feeling of disquiet filled him, the cottage so cramped that he wanted to get out. He leant forward and lightly touched Anna's shoulder.

"Come with me, my child," he said. "You belong with me. This is no place for you any longer."

Anna turned her gaze away from Karlberg, and looked up instead, a light glimmering in her eyes.

"Come," said Mr Sylvester, opening the door. The horse and trap were waiting outside, the magic carpet of the sagas, that could take her away to the land of her dreams. All she had to do was to get into it and away it would take her, away from work and toil, away from troubles and nagging and beatings and weeping.

She took one hesitant step.

"Come," said the landlord again.

He had picked up his whip and unbuttoned the cover and was now looking at her encouragingly. Now he was the wizard of the sagas with his magic wand. Abracadabra . . . and Kulla-Anna in her leather-soled socks and patched dress would disappear, to be replaced by a radiantly beautiful princess . . . Annemaria Beatrice Frederika Sylvester.

"Well, come on, then," said the landlord.

Someone whimpered. She turned her head. It was John, his eyes glowing with anguish, his lips trembling. He couldn't hear what was being said, but he understood.

"Anna . . . are you leaving us?"

She tore her eyes away from him. She didn't want to see, or feel. She wanted to leave, to go away, to go home to her land, the saga land where she was a princess . . .

One step, two steps . . . and she would be outside the door and saved.

"Anna!" cried the twins. "Don't go. Don't leave us!"

And the next second, it was as if a storm had broken out. Five pairs of arms were suddenly round her, five thin small bodies pressed and pushed against her.

"Anna-minnie, stay with us, don't go! Anna-minnie-minnie, no, don't go, don't leave us . . . Anna."

Five small white faces were raised to hers, terrified, full of anguish. "Stay with us . . . don't leave us, Anna."

The smaller children were all talking at once, frightened by something they hardly understood, something in their father's tears, in the strange man's words, in the very air around them; helpless, anguished, in need of protection. "Anna . . . Anna . . . *don't go*!"

She stood there like a young tree in the storm, a birch sapling about to break.

"Well," said Mr Sylvester impatiently.

Anna looked down at the children round her, her face pale and beads of sweat on her forehead.

"Come," said the landlord again. He had waited long enough now.

Anna ran the tip of her tongue round her dry lips, then lifted her head, looking straight at the landlord.

"Thank you most respectfully, sir," she said. "But I cannot come with you. I cannot. I have to stay here, with the children."

Mr Sylvester frowned. Then he bowed his head with a nod of understanding. With so much crying and weeping, he had to admit that it was impossible at that moment.

"We can wait a few days," he said. "I'll send a trap to fetch you."

Anna shook her head, a strand of hair slipping out of her plait at the movement and curling up by one ear.

"The promise I gave Ellen still stands," she said. "Ellen is dead, but the promise still stands. I couldn't escape that if I went to the end of the world, I assure you, sir. I must stay here and look after the children."

The landlord stood in the doorway for a minute. They looked at each other, the girl and the man. It was like a duel between them. Then the landlord again lowered his head, slowly closed the door and left. Anna shuddered . . . it had at once become so empty and cold and grey in there.

Eleven

The children came racing and splashing down the slope through the melting snow, the twins competing to be first, pushing and shoving as they tried to pass each other on the narrow path. Behind them came Addie, galloping like a foal and dragging a wooden box behind him. In the box sat the baby girl on a few tufts of hay. She still had no shoes, but Anna had started putting her in the box and letting her sit outside in it to give her a breath of fresh air and let her enjoy the spring sun. But she didn't like being left alone, so the others dragged her along with them wherever possible.

Anna was washing down by the stream, the early April sun shining down on the curls on her forehead. Pieces of ice jostled at the edge of the stream and the water was very cold. Anna's thin hands were blue and swollen, the tip of her nose blue, too. Her nose kept running so that she had to blow it on the edge of her apron. She got up hastily and held out her hands to fend off the rushing horde of children, as the stream had overflowed with the melting snow and was coursing along, strong and deep.

"Children, for heaven's sake . . . you'll go straight in and drown if . . ."

"Anna! Anna . . .!" They were all talking at once, excited

and wide-eyed. "There's a trap coming up the hill from the manor. A grand one. It's the landlord again, I expect. Perhaps he's come back to fetch you again!"

"There's two people in it," panted Addie. "One driving and one inside. I thinks it's Frans driving."

Frans was one of the estate labourers and there were many stories about his strength and brutality, so Anna's face paled.

"Oh," she mumbled. Ever since the landlord had come up the hill with the message about Ellen's death, wanting to take Anna back to the manor, she had been tormented with worry that one day she would be taken away by force. At nights she dreamt about being lifted up and carried away, while the children, terrified and helpless, ran behind crying and screaming. Not that she had anything against being a fine young lady, but her promise to Ellen could not be broken. Her heart ached whenever she thought of their helplessness and what would happen if they were without her.

"Supposing they've come to take you away . . ." they whispered again, pressing close to Anna. "Supposing Frans has been sent up to fetch you."

"Nonsense," said Anna, trying to calm them and herself with a smile that was more of a grimace. She quickly put the rinsed clothes into a pail, picked it up with one hand, grasped the washing-board firmly with the other and began struggling up the slope. There was no point in trying to hide, so she thought she'd better go and face them. She tightened her grip on the washing-board, noting that her teeth were chattering.

"It's the cold, that's all," she thought, smiling encouragingly at the children, who were tearfully clinging to her skirts. The baby in the box was whimpering too, but that was mostly because the ride uphill was not nearly such fun as the ride down.

When they came to the top, there was indeed a trap outside

the cottage, and Mademoiselle, fat and ungainly, was just in the process of untangling herself from the cover and her shawls. She landed on the ground with a thump and Anna put down the bucket of washing and went up to greet her, keeping a firm hold on the washing-board, while the children also maintained their firm grasp on her skirts.

"Good-day," she said, curtseying respectfully, and three of the children did the same, in their terror, Willie and Addie forgetting they were boys. But the babe waved her arms and squealed at the sunlight glittering on the silver on the horse's harness.

"Good-day, my child," said Mademoiselle, taking Anna's freezing little hand in her large plump one. "I've come with a message from Mr Sylvester."

"Oh, yes," said Anna, curtseying respectfully at the very sound of the name. Her heart pounded and she glanced over at Frans sitting on the box, looking grimly squint-eyed.

Mademoiselle folded her hands across her stomach and looked seriously and critically at Anna.

"You're thinner every time I see you," she said. It was like an accusation and Anna fingered her skirt in embarrassment.

"There's not much food about at this time of year," she said apologetically. "And I've always been a bit thin and scraggy, anyhow."

Mademoiselle did not reply, but simply nodded at Frans, who at once clambered down from the box. The children screamed and clung to Anna, who took a step back, clutching at the washing-board. They would never make her leave the children, never, for what would they do, left alone with no one to look after them and keep them warm and fed and get them clean clothes now and again . . .

But Frans didn't even glance in Anna's direction. He

started rummaging under the cover in the trap and hauling out a couple of sacks and a keg, which he then carried over and placed on the porch.

"They're a small gift from the landlord," said Mademoiselle. "Well, naturally I suggested it—men don't think that far, of course . . ." She stopped and looked at Anna. "You defied him," she went on. "Didn't you? That time he came to fetch you, and you stubbornly refused to go with him."

Anna straightened up, a pink patch appearing on each cheek.

"It was impossible for me to leave the children," she said, looking straight at Mademoiselle. "I have to keep my promise to Ellen."

Mademoiselle did not reply at once. When she saw that thin figure in front of her, the tears rose in her throat and she was forced to pull out her big snowy-white handkerchief and blow her nose. She blew and trumpeted and spent a lot of time polishing her nose, trying to hide her emotion. Meanwhile she remembered the conversation she had had with Mr Sylvester the day after they had gone to Kulla to fetch Anna. He had come driving back, looking both angry and sad. He hadn't said a word, but had gone straight to his room, closed the door, and there he had sat alone for the rest of that day and night. But the next morning, he had summoned Mademoiselle. When she had gone in, he had been sitting at his desk with all the photographs of Miss Annemaria in front of him.

"Mademoiselle Modig," he had said. "The girl up there at Kulla *is* my grandchild. Indeed, we have not been able to find any concrete evidence, but that girl stood there in front of me with her head up and looked at me with her strange calm eyes, and I *saw* she was Annemaria's child. *She* defied me with exactly the same stubborn calm and said: 'You can neither tempt me nor force me to break my promise to Edmund. I love him and he loves me, you must see that, Father dear.' But I said: 'You're my daughter and must obey me. *I* decide whom you shall love.' But you know, Mademoiselle, what happened. I lost her for ever. Tell me now, Mademoiselle, what shall I do with that child up there?"

Mademoiselle had thought carefully before answering. Finally, she said: "If that girl is our little Annemaria's child, then you can't force her to do what she doesn't want to do. It's no good trying to make her break her promise to Karlberg's wife. Instead, you'll have to try to make it as easy as possible for her to keep it."

Then Mr Sylvester had thrown out his hands helplessly. "But," he said. "How? I can't just let her stay up there in poverty and wretchedness."

"Poverty and wretchedness is not necessary . . . you'll have to find something to cure it," Mademoiselle had said. "You'll have to see to it that there's food and warmth and clothes, and that Karlberg has some adult help in the house, so that the girl doesn't have to work herself to death. When the children are looked after by a responsible housekeeper and have what they need, then the girl will feel free of her promise. That's the time to bring her down here."

Mr Sylvester had frowned thoughtfully in reply.

"Yes," he had said. "Perhaps you're right. But if I give Karlberg certain advantages because of Anna, then I'm being unfair to my other crofters. It'll arouse jealousy and bad blood."

Then Mademoiselle had incautiously informed him that the crofters in general were so badly off that certain changes and easing of their agreements with Mr Sylvester might well be justified. Mr Sylvester could well do something, in his mercy, for them all, she had said.

But then Mr Sylvester had grown angry and her outspokenness had been met with great disapproval. He had always been hard-hearted and the loneliness of old age had done nothing to soften him. He had never tolerated criticism and neither did he now. He had ordered Mademoiselle to leave, and then had not spoken to her for several days. But it was clear that he was suffering, and then today he had come to her and given her his orders.

"I have decided to take your advice and let the girl stay there for the time being. I realise that if I force her to leave, I would perhaps kill something good in her and she would no longer be my Annemaria's child. Go on up there, then, with whatever food you think necessary, and see to it the girl gets clothes so that she looks decent. But I want it done as discreetly as possible. I don't want envy among my subordinates."

And Mademoiselle had sighed and thought it best not to protest. She had taken Frans with her, because he was the most silent of the labourers, and driven up to Kulla. Now she was facing Anna, blowing her nose to keep her tears at bay. Just imagine . . . Annemaria's child . . . just imagine. Well, there could be no mistake. Those strange eyes, so clear and dark-blue, narrowing towards the temples. And that forehead beneath the shiny small curls. And her way of holding her head up . . . no, there could be no mistake.

But Mademoiselle also knew that a twelve-year-old child could not be fully adult in character, however wise and understanding she appeared to be, so she was afraid of putting ideas into Anna's head. It would be best to say as little as possible about her origins and all that, as long as the girl was forced to stay at Kulla.

"Well," she said. "Mr Sylvester is no longer angry with you. He's sent these to the motherless children you're looking after." She gestured towards the things Frans had put down on the porch, and Anna and the children stared at them, curtseying again. The twins took a step forward in that direction, but respect for Mademoiselle won over their curiosity, and they stayed where they were, holding on to Anna's skirt. But Addie let go the string he had been holding and crept up to take a closer look at the horse. He thought the landlord's horses were the finest in the world.

"I'd like a word with Karlberg," Mademoiselle said. "Is he home?"

Anna shook her head. Karlberg and John had gone off into the forest early that morning and were not expected back until evening. But if Mademoiselle had time to come in and wait, then . . .

Mademoiselle did not have time, but she asked Anna to pass on the message to Karlberg that there was to be no talk about the gifts. Then she showed them what was in the sacks, flour in one, potatoes in the other, and the keg was full of syrup. Anna flushed, for she had never seen so much food all at once before.

"Oh!" she gasped, curtseying several times. "Oh, goodness, come and look, children, at what we've been given! Shake hands and say thank-you, now, all of you."

She stopped suddenly with a cry, and the next moment was flying down the slope towards the stream. Addie had let go the string of the baby's box, and as it had been standing just at the top of the slope, the box had begun to slide downwards, the baby happily helping the process with lively jerks. Now the box was rushing down at such a speed that slush was flying in all directions, the passenger waving her arms about and squealing with delight.

Anna ran so that she almost fell, but she couldn't catch up

with the box. It scooted out on to the water rushing between the ice floes and was caught by the current and swirled round for a moment before tipping over. The baby's delighted squeals became an astonished gurgle, and a pair of small arms waved helplessly before vanishing. Then the box came up again and sailed on, emptied of its contents, carried along the current, small wisps of hay floating round it.

Anna kicked off her clogs and jumped. The water came up to her armpits and was so cold that for a moment she lost consciousness, the skin on her body apparently shrinking and cracking over her muscles and sinews. But the next moment she came to and struggled through the ice-floes to reach the lifeless bundle that was just floating out into midstream.

Up on the hill, they had realised what Anna's swift flight was about and had come down, the children screaming, Mademoiselle stumbling on the slippery slope and sliding the remainder of the way on her broad backside, crying out to the labourer to come and help. But Frans was occupied with the horse. It had been frightened by the screaming and was rearing and threatening to bolt. To Frans, the landlord's horse was much more important than a couple of crofter's brats.

Anna had caught hold of the baby and was trying to hold her above water as she struggled back up. The stream was not so deep that she could not stand, and if it had been summer, the whole thing would have been child's play. But the cold water took her breath away and made her movements clumsy and numbed. A floe came swirling along and knocked against her, and when her foot slid on the muddy stones at the same time, she lost her balance and vanished under the water with the baby in her arms. The children on the bank screamed and Mademoiselle rushed in with her skirts pulled up until she was knee-deep in the water. Having got that far, she realised her helplessness, her body too old, fat, clumsy and rheumaticky, the cold water stiffening her limbs. She stood in the water with her skirts up, screaming too.

Someone came racing out of the forest, a small grey, bearded creature like a troll. He plumped in to the water close to Mademoiselle, holding out a branch towards Anna, who had just appeared between the floes, and in less than a minute, it was all over, Anna on land with the baby in her arms, coughing and spitting out water, Mademoiselle standing beside her, her skirts dripping. She was staring after the old man, who had vanished like a shadow back into the forest again, a black cat following him with long graceful leaps.

"Gracious!" said Mademoiselle. "If that strange creature hadn't left real footprints in the snow behind him, I'd have thought I was seeing things."

"Gracious!" she said again, bending down to wring out her skirts. But Frans, who had at last arrived after calming down and tethering the horse, looked towards the forest and spat three times in front of him and then three times behind.

"Fie!" he said. "Fie take you, you evil thing, you."

Only Anna, running as best she could back up to the house, turned her head and called out in her clear girl's voice:

"Thanks for your help, kind sir, thanks for your help!"

When Mademoiselle got back to the cottage, Anna had already undressed the baby and was rubbing her dry with a coarse piece of sacking. The babe had come to life and was bringing up a great deal of water. She lay shivering on the sofa while Anna rubbed and massaged, her teeth chattering with compassion and anxiety.

Mademoiselle snatched the cloth from her.

"Think about yourself, now, child. Take your clothes off at

once and get yourself dry. Do as I tell you now. I'll see to the child in the meantime."

She put her plump hand on Anna's soaking back and pushed her over towards the bedroom, then turned to the baby. The baby at once came back to life. Unused to the sight of strangers and upset and frightened by what had just happened, she started yelling and struggling, her small naked body as slippery as an eel as it twisted and turned.

"Leave her until I get back," cried Anna from the bedroom, hunting feverishly for clothes. She had no more of her own, and what remained of Ellen's clothes were far too large for her.

But Mademoiselle would not give in. Goodness gracious me, was it that difficult to manage an infant! Mademoiselle was ashamed, she, who had once looked after little Annemaria, surely she could win the confidence of this shivering little bundle.

"Now, listen, little one," she pleaded, stretching out her hands. "Let's just talk about it . . . I'm quite harmless . . . ow!"

She screeched with fright and astonishment when the baby leant forward and clamped her sharp little teeth into her finger.

Mademoiselle's first instinct was to spank the child. The twins and Addie, watching open-mouthed and unable to overcome their shyness, closed their eyes in fright and pressed back against the kitchen wall at the thought of the earthquake the baby had now caused.

But Mademoiselle lowered her hand and looked thoughtfully at the child lying shivering and naked into the corner of the sofa, prepared to bite again if anything came near enough. She looked at the child for a whole minute, then turned her eyes to her bitten finger, where there were four small marks in the skin. Then she went over and opened the kitchen door and resolutely brought in the keg, thrust her finger into the clear sticky syrup and again stretched her hand out towards the baby.

As quick as a weasel the child snapped again. But the next moment she was quite still, her round blue eyes widening as she slowly sucked Mademoiselle's finger clean of syrup.

"There we are, then," said Mademoiselle, dipping her finger into the keg again.

"Mmmmm," said the baby, falling unasked into her arms, her mouth open hungrily.

When Mademoiselle finally left Anna and the children after many warnings and promises, and Frans had helped her up into the carriage, wrapped a sheepskin round her wet feet and turned the horse towards the manor again, Anna sent the twins out to fetch more wood from the shed. Then she lit the fire in the oven, fetched the dough-tray in from the porch and set about making dough from the flour. The baby was now firmly tucked up in their best sheepskin and had been given hot milk and ginger to drink. Anna herself was bustling round in an old tunic and skirt of Ellen's, fastened up with pins to stop herself tripping over it. Clothes were hanging all over the kitchen and the warmth from the fire made it a practical idea to bake today.

Anna kneaded and rolled and grew hot and sweaty working on the great pile of dough, a pleasant feeling for one who had just been in the icy water of the stream. The children crowded round with eager noses above the baking board to inhale the sweet spicy smell. The bread being made now, so sweet and good, had never before been seen on their table.

Dally-Peter's goat, still living in the corner in the other

room, came tripping out with the little grey hen on its back, butting its way through the group of children to join in. Anna put down a saucer of flour for it—never mind the waste, this was a special day. She thought about the ox and Skolla out there in the barn, too, and sent the twins with a saucer of flour for them each. On top of each heap of flour she put a dollop of syrup.

When Karlberg came in that evening, irritable and weary and hungry, an even more weary John behind him, a pile of delicious-smelling small brown loaves lay on the table, and there was a holiday atmosphere over the whole household. Karlberg sniffed loudly and stared in surprise.

'What . . . what's this?" he said, unable to believe his eyes, because for the last month there had been no flour at Kulla. Every week Karlberg had had to go down to the miller and borrow a couple of kilos 'on the slate' until times were better.

"They brought it from the manor," said Anna, standing by the fire stirring the evening porridge, warm and happy. "The landlord sent it all . . . and he says it's for the children, and we're not to talk about it," she went on.

But Karlberg was so surprised that he had to go and poke the flour sack and taste the syrup, wondering what it was all about, because never before had he heard of Mr Sylvester giving away anything to his workers, however bad things were for them. Then they sat down at the table and had porridge made of flour with syrup on it, together with the fresh bread. That night all the children went to bed with enough food inside them.

When they were all in bed and silence reigned in the cottage, Anna put on her knitted cardigan and clogs, pushed two of the best loaves into a paper bag and crept out. Silently she slipped up through the forest, the darkness beginning to thicken between the trees, the patches of snow deep among the heather. There was no light in Dally-Peter's cottage, but the porch door was unlocked. Anna pushed it open a crack and thrust the bag of bread inside.

Then she pattered silently back through the forest.

Twelve

It was marvellous what happened at Kulla. They came up from the manor every week with more flour and potatoes, salt herrings in kegs, whole pieces of pork, and butter and cheese and smoked sausages. The wagon came in the evening, unloaded on to the porch steps and silently turned back again, for the landlord was still firm about keeping his charity secret.

The empty cupboards at Kulla were soon stocked as they had never been before, and the children's pale hollow cheeks filled out and grew rosy. They had meat or cheese with their potatoes every day, while before they had had nothing but a little salt or at best some whortleberry jam. John took proper sandwiches to school every day, instead of the piece of black bread he was used to. Food was so plentiful that one day Anna took the goat on a rope and the little grey hen under her arm and went up to Dally-Peter's cottage to give them back and thank him for the loan. She thought it no longer right to keep them, as the children were now better off than the old man in his isolated cottage.

It was a fine day and the sun was out, melting the patches of snow, so Anna took all the children with her for the walk. The baby had a pair of shoes now, a present from Mademoiselle, real leather shoes, not the wooden-soled clatterers the children usually wore. It was the first time she had walked out of doors and she skipped up and down, holding Anna's hand, her squeals rising jubilantly up into the trees.

The other children were also frisky from the sun and the fine spring weather. The landlord had had a change of clothes sent up to Anna, and at the same time, Mademoiselle had also seen to it that the younger ones received something to keep them warm. Mademoiselle had a good heart beneath her plump bosom, and she was so confident of her position at the manor that she could allow herself to do things on her own accord now and again, should the occasion arise.

So today the children were dressed in thick new jackets and cardigans, and this capped everything. They leapt and danced about in the sun and the forest was filled with their happy voices. Even quiet John took a couple of skips of joy as he walked beside Anna, helping her control the goat. His freckled face under the red fringe had filled out a little, and his legs were no longer quite so painfully thin. He peered out of his deep-set eyes up at the blue sky and smiled his little turned-in smile.

"What are you thinking about, John?" said Anna, leaning over and speaking close to his ear. John's smile deepened.

"I don't know," he said. "I'm thinking about so many things at once and I feel so happy. I sometimes wonder if we haven't come a little way, after all . . . over there, you know . . . to the garden of Paradise. I wonder if . . . whether you sort of know the way, Anna, you know . . ."

"Silly," said Anna. John and his eternal Paradise. Well, it was good for anyone who could be happy from nothing but a thought. To make him even happier, she put her arm round his shoulders and said into his ear.

"You'll probably become a minister, John. I'm sure of it."

John did not reply, but just went on walking there in the sun, smiling gently.

They walked past some men working in the forest, and the children all greeted them politely. The men stopped working and looked at them in surprise. Karlberg's brats were known to be the worst brought up in the village, pale and ragged and sickly, moping round their cottage, teasing their mother, poor thing, now at rest in the churchyard. So the sight of this happy, rosy-cheeked and quite well-clad and even polite bunch of children was enough to make their eyes widen.

"Uhuh," said one of them, a large bearded man with little pig eyes, glaring at the goat and the little hen that obstinately had left Anna's arm and was again in its place on the goat's back.

"Uhuh, what's this funny procession in the middle of Saturday? And what sort of peculiar critters has Karlberg got himself, eh?"

Anna curtseyed and smiled. She told them they were Dally-Peter's goat and hen, and they had borrowed them for a while. Now they were taking them back, as they needed them no longer.

"Uhuh," said the man again, staring even harder. "Dally-Peter's goat and hen . . . did you ever hear the likes of such a thing? What's Karlberg mean having anything to do with that wicked creature?"

Anna saw the questioning look in the man's eyes.

"We were that short of food at the back end of the winter," she said. "The children were almost starving. So Dally-Peter was so kind and good enough to lend us both his goat and his hen."

"Uhuh," said the man again, trying to make out what had been said. The other men also came up and gathered in a circle round the children, gazing in amazement at the troll-goat standing there glaring at them, the hen on its back. It didn't like these great big men who looked so like Karlberg, so it butted in their direction, and they respectfully stood aside.

"What did you use them for?" one of the men said, meaning the goat and the hen.

"We milked the goat and the hen laid eggs, of course," said Anna, thinking the men stupid. "But things are fine back home now, so we don't need them any longer." The children all nodded, confirming her words, and talkative Addie pushed forward eagerly.

"We've got pork and cheese and meat," he boasted. "And new clothes and bread and syrup."

The baby began to jump up and down beside Anna crying "Sirwup! Sirwup!"

"Be quiet, children," said Anna, remembering the landlord's order that his gifts should be kept a secret. She pulled at the rope round the goat's neck, bobbed to the men and shooed the children on along the forest path.

But the big bearded man stood there for a long time, staring after them.

"Funny business," he mumbled. "Pork and cheese and meat and clothes and bread and syrup . . . and milk from that troll-goat critter. And black-magic things like that happening in the district—hm . . . hm . . ."

Thirteen

When the children arrived at Dally-Peter's cottage, he was standing outside, just as if expecting them. He looked small and crumpled, like a gnome in his grey cap, his face a shaggy mass of whiskers. Two little pearl-grey hens were pecking at his feet at the early grass just coming up between the patches of snow, and a black cat came slinking round from behind the house.

When the goat caught sight of the little old man, it let out a bleat, tore itself free from Anna and leapt happily towards him. The hen on its back flapped up with a cackle to join the other two, and they at once began to cackle, too, just like talkative females meeting unexpectedly.

Anna went over and greeted Dally-Peter respectfully.

"We've come at last," she said. "We've brought back your creatures. Thank you so much for the loan of them and the help you've been. Without it, the little one wouldn't be alive today. Thank you for your help that day down by the stream, too . . ."

She took his hairy paw in her firm young hand and curtseyed again.

"Thank you for all you've done for us. Come on, children, come and say thank-you, too." She shooed the little ones up and let them shake hands, one after another. Then she handed him a parcel she had been carrying, containing a smoked sausage and a piece of pork she had taken from the gifts the landlord had sent them. She had done so without Karlberg's knowledge, because he would perhaps have not allowed it, but her conscience was clear. The help Dally-Peter had given them was worth it and much more, she was certain.

When they set off back home again, the goat bleated uneasily, but made no sign of following them. It stood still rubbing itself up against the old man's legs. The cat leapt along with them for a while, purring contentedly when the children stroked it, but halfway home, it turned back and vanished.

The gifts of food from the manor went on coming and Karlberg basked in the landlord's favours. He was excused some of his day-work, as naturally the landlord did not wish to see Anna working among the maidservants in his own house. In addition, the landlord promised to find him a housekeeper, and that Karlberg thought was only right and just. If the landlord didn't want the orphanage child to do the chores at Kulla, then it was only right he should find someone else to do them.

"It's no more than right," he said once to Anna. "If I sees to you, then he should see to me . . . and if you one day wakes up and finds you're a grand young lady, then don't you go forgetting me, what's done so much for you and taken you in and kept you and all."

"No," promised Anna, her head whirling slightly whenever he talked like that. The only thing she was really sure of was that she would never forget her little foster-brothers and sisters.

Every Sunday afternoon, Anna put on the fine clothes Mademoiselle had sent her, scrubbed her work-soiled hands clean, combed down her fair hair with water and then went down to visit Mr Sylvester. He had given orders that she was to come to the big house every week. There Mademoiselle met her and noted with satisfaction that her narrow little face and lean body were beginning to fill out a little.

"Soon you'll begin to look like anyone else," she would say, hurriedly blowing her nose on a linen handkerchief to hide her emotion. The child was growing more and more like Miss Annemaria every day.

Then she went on to inspect Anna's clothing, here and there critically straightening the blue serge dress with the sailor collar she had had made by the dressmaker.

"Do you like wearing it?" she said.

"Yes, thank you," said Anna. She felt she was so grand she might blow away and hardly dared move in her new clothes. When you were used to clattering clogs it felt stiff and peculiar with leather boots laced right up your leg, and when she walked across the slippery floors of the manor house, she felt as if she was walking on ice.

She had tea with Mr Sylvester in the room beyond the drawing-room, sitting beside him on the sofa, feeling stiff and shy. He asked her how she was and sometimes patted her cheek. But he mostly just sat looking at her, and then his eyes looked as if he was thinking about things far back in time. There seemed to be pain in his gaze and he frowned heavily.

"Now he's thinking about *her* in there . . . Annemaria Beatrice Frederika," Anna thought, a pang of pity for him in her heart. For Annemaria Beatrice Frederika was dead and could never come back to her father. Anna wished she could say or do something to banish his melancholy.

But when the tea had been drunk, it was time to go home again, because Skolla had to be milked and the children had to have their evening meal. So she shook his hand and thanked him, and he patted her cheek again and asked her to come back next Sunday. When she walked through the drawing-room on her way out, she used to creep up and nod at the picture on the wall, where Annemaria Beatrice Frederika was looking down at her with a smile in her eyes.

"You and me," she thought. "You and me . . . we know, don't we?"

When she got back to Kulla, she hung up her fine clothes, put on her ordinary ones again and went out to the barn to do the milking. And then ordinary things took over and lasted until the next Sunday. But all the time, a picture of the girl in the white silk dress stayed in her heart and she knew that despite her promise to Ellen and despite her love for the children, it was with her that she really belonged.

"Annemaria Beatrice Frederika," she thought, and it was like a yearning in her heart.

Fourteen

One day a tall thin woman came climbing up the hill. Without knocking, she stepped inside the cottage and looked searchingly round.

"Oh, yes," she said, looking at the children at the table, where they were eating their breakfast gruel. "Oh, yes. Oh, yes . . ."

Then she went over and opened the door of the other room and looked in with short-sighted peering eyes. "Oh, yes," she said again. "Oh, yes."

Anna got up from the table, where she had been sitting with the baby on her lap, and looked with amazement at the stranger.

"Good morning," she said, curtseying to draw attention to herself. But the stranger did not hear. Instead she went into the other room and had a closer look, opening the door to the porch and the attic and glancing in inquisitively. Then she came out into the kitchen again.

"Yes," she said. "It's small, but it looks clean and tidy, what there is of it. I'll take the job, then. Yes. My name's Ida Mattson.

The children sat with their mouths open and Anna curtseyed

again, because she realised now that this was the housekeeper Karlberg had been promised.

"Please take a seat," she said politely, putting out another plate, pushing a chair up, then cutting another two slices off the syrup-loaf.

"No meat with the bread?" the stranger said, peering at the table.

Anna flushed slightly. "No," she said. "Not now, but we have some with our dinner potatoes. One has to be careful."

"Oh," said the stranger, munching gloomily at her bread. "Uhuh. You see, I've been used to better places, with the gentry and so on. When's he coming home, then, this Karlberg?"

"He's a good crofter," said Anna, thinking the situation had better be made clear from the start. "He's doing day-work for the landlord today, down at the manor."

"Oh, I see," mumbled the housekeeper with little interest. Then she fell silent and just ate. She ate all the gruel that was left in the pan and finished off most of the rest of the loaf. Then she went out and sat in the sun on the porch steps while Anna washed the dishes.

"It's nice to sit and sun yourself when you're full up," she said.

Ida Mattson seemed to like it at Kulla, but it was not the same story with the children. They did not seem to be able to get used to this new member of the family. At first they were shy, quietly tiptoeing round, because on the very first day, Ida had said firmly that she didn't want any noise indoors. John had to go out and sit on the chopping-block in the woodshed or on a bundle of straw in the barn to learn his homework, which he was used to doing out aloud, and his monotonous babbling irritated Ida.

"You'll drive a body crazy," she said. "Like a bee buzzing in your ear."

It was so quiet and still indoors that even the baby was affected by the silence. She sat in a corner, no longer even cooing to herself. But if Ida came anywhere near her or tried to pick her up, she swiftly snapped at her with her sharp little teeth.

"Gracious me!" said Ida. "What'll that child turn into, starting life like that? Like a wildcat, she is. Needs a good beating to stop that, before it's too late."

The twins were bewildered and Addie's cheeks seemed to droop, as if he were miserable about something. Although Ida had taken on the cooking, spending all day frying things at the stove, and they had fried bread and pork and sausage morning, noon and night, the children lost their appetites and grew thinner. Anna found it difficult to get her food down, too, and she was uneasy over the way Ida treated the gifts from the manor. All her twelve-year-life, Anna had had it impressed on her that you had to be economical with what you had and always use things cautiously. But Ida put so much butter in the frying pan for pancakes, there was none left for their bread the next day. And at one weekly baking, she scraped the syrup-keg so bare, the next week she had to bake with nothing but flour and water.

"Oh, I expect they'll send some more," she said, peering down the hill. Karlberg seemed to be in agreement with Ida. He had always grumbled and complained about Anna's bad housekeeping, and now he relished the plentiful supply of food. He ate, smacking his lips, put double slices of cheese on his bread, and demanded pork and sausages and brawn in his sandwich bag when he was out on day-work. He grew fat and bloated, and began to think it a nuisance to have to work. He had to work his agreed days down on the manor farm, but his own work on the croft he took more and more light-heartedly. The spring ploughing was neglected, some patches remaining unploughed and the seeds not deep enough in the soil. Instead, he sat in the kitchen drinking coffee with Ida, and in the evenings as it grew dark, he went out to wait for the next delivery from the manor.

"If I keep the girl, then it's right that the landlord keeps me," he said again, belching noisily from his bloated stomach.

But rumours began to go round the district that Dally-Peter's goat was giving money instead of milk and the hen was laying golden eggs for Karlberg, so that he was now so well off, he had no need to work.

It was full spring now and the slopes round Kulla were covered with white anemones. The grass was tall and rich between the boulders, so the ox and Skolla had good grazing. Their scraggy bodies slowly regained strength and their hides shone and glowed from the daily brushing Anna gave them. Anna still looked after the animals on the days Karlberg worked for the manor. Mademoiselle had told him that the landlord had said that Anna was not to do any more heavy work, but when Skolla stubbornly and angrily refused to allow Ida to milk her, turning unruly and kicking out as soon as she came into the barn, there was no alternative but for Anna to continue.

Skolla and Ida came up against each other on the very first day. The animals had long been used to Anna's soft hands and her clear young voice greeting them every morning with friendly words.

"Hullo, critters mine . . . morning Skolla-lolla, Lolla-horn, Buttercup . . . and morning to you, old ox-man mine, morning, morning . . ." was what they were used to hearing when the door opened every morning. And Skolla and the ox would turn their heads and stare expectantly at the small figure in clogs clattering across to them.

"Mooooo," Skolla would say, which meant good morning and welcome.

"Muuooo," the ox would low, hoarser and rougher than the cow, but just as well meant.

"Thank you, both," said the voice that understood their language perfectly.

Then there would always be a pat and little scratching between their horns, however much of a hurry she was in, and the friendly feel of those hands was something for the two creatures to dream about all day.

Then one morning the door crashed open with a screech and a tall stranger came striding in with the milk pail in one hand and stool in the other. She walked straight up to Skolla and thumped her with the stool.

"Move over, wretch, so I can get at you," a sharp irritable voice said, and a shudder ran through both animals.

They turned and glared, Skolla unable to move out of sheer dismay. So she received another and harder blow from the stool.

"Well, come on then . . . move over, now."

Then Skolla moved out of sheer astonishment and shock. The stool was put down with a thump and the tall female sat on it with the pail between her knees. A pair of hard unfriendly hands grasped Skolla's teats.

Then Skolla reacted. This was all wrong. Something was wrong. Wrong voice, wrong hands, everything wrong. She lifted her tail and struck. It was meant as a warning, rather than out of malice, a means of attracting attention. Something was wrong.

The tail swept into Ida's face, angering her. She kicked the cow hard with her clog. "Stand still, wretch!"

The hard unfriendly fingers squeezed again. "Look now, stand still, or else . . ." Skolla turned her head, glared and snorted. This new person smelt bad, a smell as unpleasant as her hands and voice. There was something wrong. She should be a small fair child with gentle hands and a clear chirping voice. Something was *very* wrong.

Skolla lifted her leg and struck backwards with all her strength. Ida dropped the milk pail into the muck channel and screamed.

"Wretched creature. . . !" She grabbed the stool and struck the cow as hard as she could. Skolla kicked again, beside herself with pain and fear. The ox was frightened too, and began jerking at his chain and bellowing. Ida struck and shouted to bring the wretch to order and the barn was filled with shrieks and bellows, the rattle of chains and thumps of blows that Ida was delivering in all directions.

Suddenly Skolla got loose. The rotten old rope she had been tethered by had been broken by her wild jerks. Skolla backed out of her stall and turned her horns on Ida.

"Booooooo," she said, and there was neither softness nor melancholy in the voice this time, but she sounded as hoarse and as rough as a bull. "Booooooo."

Ida dropped the stool and ran, and Skolla picked it up on her horns in passing and ran after her. Ida screamed and Skolla bellowed in reply. Halfway to the cottage, Ida caught the milking-stool full in her back and fell flat on her face. It could have been really serious if Anna and the children had not come rushing out to help, because Skolla was wild and agitated and just about to attack again.

Anna rushed up with the broom and hit Skolla between her horns to bring her back to her senses.

"Skolla, love, golden horns, Buttercup . . . what's the matter with you?" she cried.

At the sound of that familiar and much-loved voice, Skolla's rage vanished immediately. She stopped, snorted in Ida's direction and shook her head with its long horns. Then she tripped over and thrust her nose into her Anna's armpit.

"Moooo," she said, now the usual slightly sorrowful sound of longing again. "Mooo!"

Then she allowed herself to be led back to her stall and Anna picked up the overturned pail, rinsed it out, fetched the stool to sit on and then drew the milk from the taut udder in her usual way. Skolla stood still and began to chew contentedly, now and again turning her head to stare at Anna with shining eyes.

"Mooo?" she said, almost like a question.

"Yes, yes, my friend," said Anna.

But since then, Ida could not go into the barn without the animals turning restless and starting to stamp and bellow. Karlberg ordered Anna to keep the cow calm and stand by her head while Ida did the milking, so the animal would gradually get used to her. Then Skolla stood quite still while Anna talked to her and stroked her, but she would give no milk.

"She's keeping it back, the wretch," said Ida, pulling and squeezing as hard as she could, but in the end she got up off the stool and handed over to Anna.

"You're the one who's turned the heads of the animals and the brats in this place," she said crossly. "I can see that it's you that's done it. Go on and get on with it, as you're the cause of it all, girl."

So Anna continued to do all the chores on the croft, relieved only of the cooking. But she did not mind and neither did she complain. And Ida Matsson had the chores done for her, so enjoyed her job as Karlberg's housekeeper.

Fifteen

One day, the schoolmaster sent a message with John to say that now there was some adult help at Kulla, Anna should go to school for the last few weeks of term. Anna was pleased, because during the time that Ellen's illness and death had kept her away from school, she had often silently longed to go. She had also tried to steal brief moments of reading with John, to keep up with what he was learning at school. But Karlberg muttered and mumbled, saying school was no use to Anna.

"What good will that do?" he said. "Either you'll always be a poor servant, and then all you needs to know is how to get up potatoes and scrub floors. Or else you'll be a grand miss and get them to keep you, and then you don't need to know nothing. Silly nonsense, saying you got to go to school, when you're wanted back here."

But as Mr Bromander and the school governors had decided, Karlberg had no choice, and Anna put on the blue spotted calico dress that had recently been sent up to her, tied her kerchief round her fair hair and went off to school with John.

That day was bright and friendly, quite different from the first time she had stepped over the school threshold. That day was a confirmation that life had taken a turn for the better for Anna. It began with the trap from the manor passing them.

Mr Sylvester himself was driving, and when he saw the two children, he reined in the horse.

"Well, this is a good meeting," he said, his voice cheerful. "Up you get, youngsters, and you can have a ride."

Anna curtseyed and John bowed, then both climbed up beside him, John, the shyest, sitting furthest out and Anna between him and Mr Sylvester. The latter looked at her:

"My child," he said. "I've been thinking a great deal about you this week. I have had good news from abroad through a firm of lawyers I assigned the task of tracing your ancestry. They have found a clue, perhaps even confirmation that we really are related."

"Oh, yes," said Anna, politely, smiling to herself. Mr Sylvester always talked such a lot about papers, evidence, lawyers and other strange and complicated things. Every time they met he always had something of that kind to say. Sometimes he said it seemed impossible to find evidence, and then he was sad and absent-minded. Then on other days, like today, he was more hopeful about all those papers and evidence, and his mood at once changed. It was hard to understand, but perhaps it was always difficult to understand such a grand old gentleman like him. Anna smiled to herself. *She* knew. She didn't need any papers. She knew, anyhow.

"You and me," she thought, seeing the picture of Annemaria Beatrice Frederika in her mind, "you and me, we *know*, don't we?"

"I'm going away," Mr Sylvester went on. "I may even have to go abroad to acquire certain papers in person, so I'll be away for some time. But I want you to continue your weekly visits to the manor house, so that Mademoiselle Modig knows that you are well and all is in order. A young relative of my late wife's, Miss Regine, who knows the manor well, will be in charge of the house and servants in my absence. If you want anything special, then you must turn to her. Have you understood, my child?"

"Yes," said Anna, an ache in her heart at the thought of Mr Sylvester going away. She would not see him on Sundays as before. She glanced sideways at him. His face looked less stern today, and the lines on his forehead were almost absent. That was probably thanks to those old papers. Old men like him perhaps had to have written words on paper to be happy. Anna suddenly realised how much she wished he would find the papers he wanted, for his own sake.

"Though we . . . we know, us two," she thought, smiling again at the picture within her.

Mr Sylvester was silent for a long time, but then he suddenly seemed to remember something.

"Tell me," he said. "The new housekeeper . . . does she like it at Kulla? And do you like her?"

Anna hesitated, looking to John for help. But John had not heard and so had nothing to say.

Mr Sylvester turned to her.

"Well . . .?"

"Yes," said Anna in a low voice. "I think she likes it."

"Well, that's good," said the landlord, and that was the end of it.

They drove past groups of schoolchildren, who all gaped in surprise. John waved at them and smiled. His freckled cheeks were pink with happiness. Just imagine—riding to school with the landlord himself!

Mr Sylvester happened to turn his eyes towards him and saw his radiant expression. Against his will, he was moved and felt a need to say a few friendly words.

"Well," he said. "You who're Karlberg's eldest son, I

suppose you'll be the one to take over the croft after him. Is that right, boy?"

John's face turned scarlet, because he could see the landlord's lips moving, but not hear what he was saying. But Anna came to his rescue.

"John's a little deaf," she said apologetically. "You have to speak into his ear. But I can tell you that he isn't very suited to being a crofter."

She leant over towards John.

"John!" she cried. "The landlord wants to know what you're going to become when you're grown up. Tell him what you want to be, John."

John dared a glance at the landlord and nervously pushed his hair away from his forehead.

"Anna says I'd make a good minister," he said, smiling shyly. "And if that's so, then . . ."

"Then you're going to be one," the landlord said, with a laugh. "So you think it's just a matter of *being* one, do you?"

Anna straightened up. She had sensed the note of contempt in Mr Sylvester's voice. She raised her eyes and looked straight at him.

"Greatgran, who's dead now, always said that anyone who longs enough will find his way in the end," she said. "And John's heart is full of longing. He dreams and talks all the time about his Garden of Paradise."

Mr Sylvester stopped laughing and looked at the two beside him. He had had very little to do with children in his life, in fact had always avoided such irritations. His interest in Anna lay only in the possibility of there being family ties between them. But now he was amused against his will.

"His paradise," he said. "What is that?"

"It's John's heaven," said Anna.

"He has his own heaven, has he? Well, I'm . . ."

"It's no ordinary heaven," said Anna. She was still sitting stiffly, because she had seen the smile playing round the landlord's thin lips and she wanted him to know that this was no joke. One just did not joke about the Garden of Paradise.

"The Garden of Paradise," said Mr Sylvester, trying to appear serious. "It sounds fine. I can see it's no ordinary heaven. Tell me, where is it?"

Anna bent over John again.

"Mr Sylvester is asking the way to the Garden of Paradise, John," she cried.

At that moment, the trap stopped outside the schoolhouse and John had no time to reply. Mr Bromander, seeing the arrival of the trap, came running out to ask Mr Sylvester what he wanted. The landlord patted John on the head and stroked Anna's cheek.

"You can tell me about it another time," he said, turning to Mr Bromander.

The two children jumped down from the trap and Anna curtseyed and John bowed in thanks for the ride. Then they crossed the school yard, where the other children were standing staring at the trap.

Anna went to greet each of them, as she had not been to the school for a whole term.

"Hullo, Rosa," she said. "Hullo, Viola, May, Lisa . . . Hullo, Stina . . ."

Last of all in the line was Linnea, a bitter look in her eyes when she saw the fair curls on Anna's forehead and the new blue-spotted dress.

"Hullo, Kulla-Anna," she said mockingly.

But Anna smiled at her in the same way as she had to the others.

"Hullo, Linnea," she said.

When they were at their desks inside the schoolroom, Mr Bromander came up and gave Anna a friendly pat on her shoulder with his cane. Then he took her right through the catechism, the bible, geography and history to see how much she had forgotten during her long absence. When she managed to answer all the questions without faltering, he was so delighted that he had to give her another pat with the end of his cane.

"See, see," he chuckled with satisfaction. "Sometimes it is really worth while being a schoolmaster . . ."

When he had noted that Anna had grown quite a bit, that her face had filled out and her limbs grown stronger, he shook his cane in the direction of the desk where Karl was sitting, glowering under his fringe.

"Just you watch out for your nose, now," he said. "Because I can see from Anna, that she understands your language better than ever now."

They all burst out laughing, as they knew what the schoolmaster meant. Karl was always fighting, and blows and thumps had become his way of expressing himself. So they all disliked him and took the chance now of laughing as loudly as they could.

But Anna felt sorry for Karl, sitting there with his cheeks scarlet with shame, because she thought what was past was past and there was no need to mention it any longer.

"I think we've stopped talking that way," she said gently.

Sixteen

It was a good day, that first day back at school, but when they got back home, they were once again faced with a bunch of crying, sniffing children.

"Oh, Anna, Anna," they cried, running towards her. "We've been waiting for so long for you. We've been waiting for *ages* . . . Oh, Anna, please don't go away from us again . . ."

They clung to her, sobbing and crying into her skirt, complaining about Ida. Addie and the baby had both been beaten with the broom and had red patches on their backsides to show for it. And the twins had been turned outside with no dinner because they had behaved badly during the day.

Anna comforted and calmed them as they slowly made their way up the last slope towards the cottage, the children clinging to her skirts. Ida was standing in the doorway, waiting, her arms akimbo and her eyes glowering. She was angry and upset, too. The children had behaved very badly all day and Skolla had attacked her when she had gone out to the meadow to milk her. Then Skolla had run off into the forest.

"Folk and critters is both crazy in this place," she said, glaring accusingly at Anna. "And it's you, girl, what's the cause of it all. Now you just go and undo what you've done, and go and find that wretched cow, too."

There was no answer to that, so Anna silently took off her blue spotted dress, hung it up, put on her everyday clothes, took a cup of coffee and a slice of bread standing up, and then set off to search in the forest. John wanted to come with her, but she asked him to stay at home to look after the children, who kept glancing furtively at Ida, pleading with Anna to stay at home with them.

The forest smelt of resin and linnea, the warmth of the sun still between the trees. Anna pattered along in her bare feet over the moss and heather and pine-needles, listening and calling.

"Skolla . . . Skolla-mine . . . yoo-hoo."

But the forest was huge and Skolla could have run anywhere. Anna decided in the end to take the route to Dally-Peter's cottage and ask his advice. He seemed to know more than most people, and perhaps he could help her.

But today the little old man wasn't waiting outside. The cottage was quite dark and silent, the front patch bare and empty. Neither the bleating of the goat nor the cackling of the hens disturbed the silence. The evening sky rose violet-blue above the hill behind the cottage.

Anna stood still listening. There was no sound except the sighing of the wind in the treetops. Perhaps Dally-Peter was away or had gone to bed, she thought, and she was just about to go on when the cat came gliding out of the forest. It leapt over to her and rubbed against her legs, miaowing. When Anna leant down to stroke it, she saw that it was nothing but skin and bone.

"Oh, oh!" she said. "What's happened, pussy?"

"Miaow!" replied the cat, miserably. Then it leapt away from her, up on to the steps, miaowing again as it clawed the closed door.

"No," said Anna. "I can't let you in. Cats like you should be out at night."

She began to walk on, as she couldn't waste time with a cat when she had to find the cow before it got dark. But the cat soon came after her, weaving round her legs and miaowing miserably.

"What a noise!" said Anna. She stopped and beckoned it to her. "Come on, pussy, come with me for a while. Then you won't be so lonely. Come on, pussy."

But the cat did not want to go with her. It ran back to the cottage again and sat on the porch looking at Anna, its eyes glinting in the half-light.

"Miaow!" it said again, as if pleading.

"What's the matter?" said Anna, suddenly aware that there was something odd about the cat's behaviour. "What do you want me to do?"

"Miaow!" cried the cat. Then it jumped up again and began clawing at the door, even trying to reach the handle.

Anna went over and felt the door. It was unlocked as usual. She pushed it open cautiously and let the cat in.

"Can't be helped," she mumbled. "When you ask like that . . ."

She stood still, her hand on the handle, uneasily aware that the stillness in and around the cottage was peculiar. The cat's eyes glowed at her from the darkness inside the cottage.

"Miaow!"

"What're you saying?" Anna took a step inside and looked. "Oh!" she cried, when she saw the mess in there. The table by the window had been tipped over and a chair lay broken beside it. There was broken china on the floor and when she tried to avoid it, her foot felt something sticky. Surprised, she lifted her foot and looked.

"Oh!" she cried. "It's blood."

She hurried over to the mantelpiece where matches were usually kept, found a bundle and quickly struck one.

"Dally-Peter, Dally-Peter . . . where are you?"

"Miaow!" said the cat from over in a corner where there was something large and dark like a bundle.

"Oh, gracious!" Anna was there in a flash, holding up the lighted match. Dally-Peter was lying there, tied up like a parcel, a sack over his head. Anna pulled him out on to the floor and tugged at the ropes to free him. She was so upset she quite forgot to be frightened.

"Oh, Dally-Peter, oh . . . what've they done to you . . . who could have done this to you . . . oh, how could they, how could they?"

She was crying with dismay and pity and anger.

"Are you alive . . . or are you dead? Tell me, please say something. . . !"

She got him up on to the sofa-bed. He was small and light, almost like a child. She lit another match and held it over him.

"Tell me you're alive. Please say you're not dead . . ."

There was a faint whimper in reply from the old man, and the light from the match was reflected in two points in the middle of all those tangled whiskers. He *wasn't* dead. He was alive and was looking at her.

"Wwww . . . water," he whispered.

"Oh, yes, of course." Anna looked round. There was an overturned bucket by the hearth and she grabbed it and ran out. She remembered the spring that ran down by the edge of the forest, and she ran to it as fast as she could, buttercups and wild chervil rustling round her feet.

When she got to the spring, someone had got there before

her and was quenching her thirst in the clear water, slurping and snorting—a pair of large eyes turned towards her in the dim light.

"Moooo," said Skolla, a little shamefacedly.

"Oh, so *there* you are, critter . . ." Anna hadn't time to be pleased at having found Skolla so easily. She pushed the cow aside to fill her bucket. "There . . . out of my way, you wretch. No, no, don't push like that . . . I must hurry and get some water."

When Dally-Peter had drunk a few mugs of water, and she had washed the dried blood from the wound on his head and bandaged it up as best she could with some strips torn from her petticoat, he perked up and could speak again.

"They took me goat . . . and me hens," he said, shaking his head. "They hit me on the head with a stone and tied me up. And then they took me goat and me hens. Oh, oh, oh, me goat and me little hens."

"Miaow!" wept the cat in confirmation, from the foot of the bed.

"Who did?" said Anna, frightened. She had opened the door to let in more light. It was dark inside the cottage with its one and only window covered with flyspots and spider's webs. She was trying to tidy and clean up a bit. "Did you see who it was, before they put the sack over your head?"

The old man went on whimpering, rocking back and forth.

"Oh, oh, oh, I was sitting there in the sun . . . thinking about nothing, neither good nor evil. Then they crept up and hit me on the head. And just as I was going off, I heard me goat bleating and crashing round the cottage . . . she didn't want to be taken, oh, no . . . oh, oh, oh."

He suddenly stopped.

"Get me some food, will you, girl?" he said. "And some for

the cat and the hedgehog. I've been here for days with a sack over me head, several days and several nights . . ."

"Oh." Anna put down the broom she had been sweeping with. "How stupid of me! Can't see further than my nose . . ."

She went over to the cupboard by the hearth and found a loaf, which she broke for the old man. Then she took the water-bucket and went out again.

"Skolla . . . Skolla-mine . . ."

Skolla's large body appeared out of the shadows of the trees and came towards her. When Anna knelt beside her and quickly began to milk her, the cow at once began to chew contentedly on the cud.

"Yes, yes," said Anna, patting her hindquarters. "You knew what you were doing when you ran off today, didn't you, old golden-horns . . ."

The bucket filled to the top with frothy warm milk, and Dally-Peter and the cat drank as much as they were able to. On the old man's orders, Anna poured some into a saucer and put it out on the porch for the hedgehog and the grass-snake.

"People call him a troll and spit when they hear his name or see him," thought Anna. "But animals seem to be at one with him . . . and he thinks about them in the middle of his own misery."

She stood still in the doorway watching the hedgehog creeping out of the grass, at once scenting the sweet milk, then she went back in and set about the cleaning again.

The old man had stopped moaning and was sitting up, his whole gnome-like little body covered with tangled hair and grey beard, and his hairy crooked fingers over his eyes. Anna glanced at him with a look of pity.

"Are you crying, Dally-Peter?"

He raised his head, his eyes blinking hard as if he were making a great effort to see and clear them.

"You disturb me, little girl," he said. "Go and sit out on the porch till I'm ready. I must see where my goat is. And my three little hens. But your heart and soul take my strength away . . . it's like that with the innocent. Go on out then, and stay there till I calls you."

Again he put his paw-like hands over his eyes, hunching down and seeming to become smaller, sitting there as immobile as a mossy tree stump.

Anna looked at him in surprise for a second, then went out and sat on the porch as he had told her to. The summer night now lay violet-covered over the forest and the grass was wet with dew. She drew her bare legs up under her skirt for warmth and watched the hedgehog, still lapping up milk from the saucer. Further away, Skolla was still faithfully waiting. Wherever she moved there was a faint clang of the bell round her neck. The black cat came soundlessly out of the cottage, leapt on to Anna's lap, curled up and began to purr. Anna absently stroked its back as she waited.

The sun was shining in her face when she woke. It had just risen above the forest line and its slanting rays were reflected in the cottage window-pane, clean now of the dirt and cobwebs. The cat had gone from her lap and there was no sign of Skolla. The hedgehog's saucer was empty.

Anna rose and went into the cottage. There was a fire in the hearth under a three-legged coffee pot, and the room was quite clean and tidy. Dally-Peter was sitting on a chopping-block in the corner by the hearth, grinding coffee-beans in a mortar. If it hadn't been for the bandage round his head, Anna would have thought she had dreamt it all.

Dally-Peter poured the ground coffee into the pot and the

good smell of coffee spread through the cottage. Anna's stomach rumbled and she realised she was hungry. Quickly she drank the mug of coffee and ate the piece of bread the old man gave her, then thanked him with a bob.

"If you don't need me any more, then I think I'd better get back . . . they're probably waiting back home and wondering where I am. And anyhow, I think that critter's gone and run away again. She's not out there."

The old man looked over the rim of his cup.

"The cow's waiting for you outside the barn door back there," he said. "And thanks you shall have for what you did last night. Now I'm wondering if you'll do me a favour, and go past Simon's place on your way home and help me goat and hens out of his woodshed. All you need do is take the hook off and open the door . . ."

Anna looked at him with respect.

"Yes, I'll do that," she promised.

The old man went with her out on to the porch.

"If you happens to meet him, that Simon, then you can give him me regards and say: *What's falsely taken is soon lost.*"

Anna bobbed again.

"I'll do that," she said obediently.

Seventeen

Simon had a croft like Kulla, and it lay a little further up towards the forest. Simon the crofter was the tall bearded man Anna and the children had met that morning in the forest, when they were returning the goat and hens to their owner. Anna worried about him as she slipped along the forest paths. Just the thought of such a wicked creature as a thief and murderer disturbed and frightened her.

No one seemed to be up and about yet at the croft, but there was a cow grazing behind the barn and a few hens on the muckheap. Anna looked at them.

"Simon's got both a cow and hens," she thought. "So he had no need to go and steal from a poor old man like Dally-Peter."

She went round the barn and found a door with a big hook on it. It was so tight she had to find a stone to shift it. As she hammered, she heard the sound of light hooves uneasily stamping about inside.

The door opened and she peered inside.

"Are you there, Fia?"

"Baaaaa!" came somewhat anxiously from inside, and when Anna had got used to the darkness, she saw the goat was tied up in one corner. Three frightened hens were standing clucking on a heap of wood. Anna went over and freed the goat and the three little hens at once flapped cackling down and settled on her back as if they knew that this was a moment to move quickly.

With a delighted bleat, the three hens in a row on her back, the goat scampered through the door and with her head high, disappeared into the forest.

Anna closed the door carefully, replacing the hook before leaving. She had already got past the cottage and was well on her way down the slope without being seen and was just about to climb over the stile into the forest, when a man came out on to the porch and called out to her.

"Hey you there, girl. Wait a moment!"

Anna glanced up towards the cottage. It was Simon himself, standing there on the porch, newly awake and scratching his beard.

"Come here a moment, girl!"

Anna got down from the fence and went slowly back up to him, her cheeks pale with fear, but she did not run away. Anyhow, she had Dally-Peter's message to pass on.

"Good morning," she said, curtseying after a quick discussion with herself as to whether thieves required the same politeness as ordinary decent people.

Simon yawned hugely in reply, his mouth large and red in the middle of his bushy black beard. He scratched his head with both hands, as at this time of the morning the lice were at their most active and lively.

"What are you doing, running round the forest at this time of the morning?" he said, yawning again.

"Our cow ran away," said Anna, hardly daring to look at that gaping mouth, which seemed as if it might swallow her whole. "I've been searching all morning, ever since it got light. I wondered if she'd been around here?"

"No," said Simon, without interest, scratching and rubbing at his hair. "I've not seen no cow. But listen, girl!" He stopped scratching and took a step nearer. "There's something I want to ask you. And I'll give you a whole twenty-five öre if you answer me question truthfully." He was whispering and looking anxiously around, as if afraid someone might be listening. "Tell me, girl. That troll-goat you borrowed last winter. And those little grey hens. Was there something special you had to do or say to get them to give what you wished. Or what, eh?"

Anna stared at him wide-eyed, not understanding what he meant.

"Hrrm," said Simon, clearing his throat impatiently. "Doesn't you understand me, girl? I asks you what you did with the goat to get it to give money. And the hens to lay gold eggs. I'll give you *two* twenty-five öre bits . . . yes, *three*, even, if you answers me honestly."

Anna shook her head, more surprised than afraid now.

"At home the goat gave milk and the hen eggs, just like any other. Gold eggs and money? What sort of nonsense is that? That kind of thing only happens in fairy tales." She couldn't help laughing at him, although he was a thief.

But Simon was not convinced. He stepped a little closer again. "I'll give you a whole krona if you'll tell."

Anna moved cautiously backwards.

"All I can tell you is what Dally-Peter said—he asked me to tell you that *what's falsely taken is soon lost.*

"Hrrm . . . what?" said Simon, staring at her.

"What's falsely taken is soon lost," repeated Anna, hurriedly curtseying. "Goodbye, now."

At which she turned round and skirts flying, she rushed away towards the safety of the forest. But as she clambered over the stile, she glanced back and saw Simon still standing there by his cottage, scratching his head. He had got straight out of bed and come out, and had no idea the stolen animals were by this time back with their owner. He was standing there puzzling over Anna's words, thinking perhaps they were a magic formula that would make the goat give money instead of milk and the hens lay gold eggs.

"Well, well," thought Anna. "Just you puzzle that out, and make sure the words stick in your head, too."

When Anna got back to Kulla, Skolla was standing outside the barn door just as Dally-Peter had said. Karlberg came out on to the porch looking cross.

"Don't know what you get up to these days, girl," he said irritably. "You seem to do just what you pleases. Here you are, running around the forest all night and the cow has to find its own way back as best it can. I'll have to do something about you . . ."

Anna did not reply. She knew Karlberg now, and knew he grumbled and muttered and mumbled largely out of habit. She shoved Skolla into her stall and before fetching the stool and bucket, gave the cow and the ox their usual morning pat. And when they turned their heads and looked at her with their shining eyes, she felt so warm and good, she had to smile.

"Old things, you two, old friends," she said.

Eighteen

As usual, Anna went down to the manor house on the following Sunday afternoon. As she was walking across the front gravel, she saw Mademoiselle standing on the veranda, a slim, dark lady in riding habit and long black boots beside her.

"Come here, child," Mademoiselle called. Anna went over to them and curtseyed shyly. She was wearing the blue-spotted dress, had combed her hair flat and was clean and tidy. As always when her hair was a little damp, it curled up round her forehead, and her face was sunburnt and rosy and soft.

Mademoiselle gave her a satisfied look and steered her over towards the stranger.

"This is the child there's so much talk about," she said, folding her plump hand across her stomach. "Tell Miss Regina what your name is, now, child," she went on, nodding towards Anna.

"My name's Annemaria Beatrice Frederika, though I'm usually called Anna," said Anna, and Mademoiselle nodded with satisfaction at each of the three names, glancing at the strange lady as if to say "There, now, what did I say?"

But the stranger did not in any way appear to share Mademoiselle's satisfaction. She looked Anna up and down with her dark blank eyes and her bold face with its protruding nose and thin, narrow mouth did not move. Then she shrugged her shoulders boyishly.

"Naturally it seems peculiar with those names," she said. "With a little imagination, there is great scope for the strangest of guesses."

"But the similarity . . . the similarity . . . can't you see it, Miss Regina?" cried Mademoiselle, in her eagerness forgetting her usual caution in Anna's presence. "Don't you see how like this child is to the child in the portrait in there, almost like the same people, Miss Regina. Come and look. Come in and have a look!"

She hustled Anna in with her into the house, through the hall and the study and into the drawing-room. There she placed Anna below the portrait in the ray of sunlight coming through the window, undid her plait so that her fair curls fell out and framed her face, placing one arm on the arm of the sofa and turning her head so that it was in the same position as the girl's in the portrait.

"Now, look!" she said triumphantly. "Look, Miss Regina. What have you got to say now?"

Miss Regina looked dutifully, and when her dark eyes met Anna's blue ones, for a brief moment they turned away in fear. The stern features paled and almost imperceptibly, she sharply drew in her breath.

But the next moment she had regained her composure and a wry smile appeared on her lips.

"With a little imagination, all fair-haired and blue-eyed children would look alike," she said, slapping her riding crop lightly against her boot. "But the girl's pretty, there's no doubt about that. Truly pretty. Uncle's probably started taking to children in his old age. Well, nothing wrong with that, but no doubt this trip abroad will be a disappointment to him.

Well, that's enough, now. Take the girl in for tea and cakes or whatever it is she usually has, but I don't want her here in the drawing-room, Mademoiselle. She smells of the barn and croft brats always have fleas. She can sit in the kitchen, and you must have the floor washed thoroughly when she's gone. I'm going riding for a while now . . . send one of the maids to get my horse brought round will you?"

At that she turned on her heel and left the room. Mademoiselle could do nothing but obey her orders.

But Anna, left behind, looked confusedly after them as she slowly plaited up her hair again.

"She didn't like me," she thought. "She didn't like me. I saw it in her eyes."

Mademoiselle came back and took her out to the kitchen to have tea, for however long she had been in service at the manor, she did not dare disobey Miss Regina. Miss Regina was only a distant relative of the landlord's wife, but everyone knew that she would one day inherit the property and the fortune, as there was no hope of his own child, Annemaria Beatrice, being alive.

"Perhaps things'll change now," thought Mademoiselle, allowing herself a little malice. She found it as difficult to like Miss Regina as it had been easy to love Miss Annemaria, in the days when Miss Regina visited the manor and had been a trial to all the servants. She was hard and unbending, and the maids, fearing her temper, used to say with a shudder that the day Miss Regina finally became mistress of the house would be the moment to ask permission to leave.

"But things'll change now, things'll change," Mademoiselle mumbled again, her plump hand running fondly over Anna's fair head. "If God is just, then in time there'll be another mistress here."

But Anna sat at the table enjoying the cakes and Mademoiselle's friendliness. She was not at all hurt by having to sit in the kitchen. The manor house kitchen, with its shining copper and light walls was the finest place in the world, and as far as smelling of the barn and having fleas, she knew that was so, because anyone dealing with animals was never quite free of such things. All she felt sad about was the memory of that look in the strange lady's eyes.

One afternoon a few days later, she met Miss Regina again. The children had been out all day gathering firewood in the forest, and Anna was chopping up branches and sticks. John was soon tired by physical activity, so had sat down to rest for a moment on the sawing-horse, while the baby was wandering about on the grassy slope, picking the heads off flowers. Addie's and the twins' voices could be heard from in among the trees, where they had come across Dally-Peter's cat and were playing with it.

Then suddenly there was someone on horseback beside them, having apparently appeared out of the ground. The horse's hooves made no sound on the grass, and as John heard badly and Anna was chopping, neither had noticed anyone coming. Miss Regina sat there on her horse watching them for a long time, before she let her riding crop fall lightly on Anna's back.

Anna had been holding the axe with both hands because of its weight, and at the touch, she jumped.

"Oh," she said, turning her head suddenly. The axe slipped and the sharp edge crashed into the ground just next to her bare foot.

Miss Regina remained sitting there, smiling and unmoved.

"You should pay a bit more attention to your work," she said. "That was a very close thing."

Anna pulled her foot to her and wiggled her big toe to make really sure it was not injured. Then she picked up the axe, placed it carefully on the block and curtseyed in greeting.

"Good afternoon," she said.

Miss Regina did not answer, as it was not her habit to greet the servants and her subordinates. She sat there silently looking round, and at that moment the children came out of the forest, Dally-Peter's cat playfully leaping ahead of them.

The children stopped in surprise when they saw the rider, as it was a very rare occurrence for any of the gentry to stray as far up as their croft. The cat stopped suddenly and glared with its green eyes at the stranger on the horse.

"Ugh!" said Miss Regina. She was a fervent hunter with a deep-rooted dislike of cats, which she considered took young hares and birds from the forest. She leant down and slashed at the cat with her crop.

"Ugh . . . get away . . . ugh, you horrid animal!"

The cat leapt aside to avoid the blow, then crouched down hissing. Miss Regina struck at it again.

"Didn't I say I wanted no cats on the estate!" she cried in annoyance. "You wretched crofters, will you never do as you're told!"

"It's not our cat," said Anna, her voice trembling, hoping the cat would have the sense to flee to the safety of the forest.

But it didn't. It stared straight at Miss Regina with its glowing green eyes, and every time the crop swept through the air, it leapt aside and hissed, the hair along its back straight up and its tail as thick as a bottle-brush. The children, terrified, staring at the strange sight, slowly began to cry, but the baby, too small to respect this grand lady as the others did, stamped her small foot and cried shrilly:

"Nice pussy . . . leave nice pussy alone . . . silly, silly, you . . . !"

"Horrible animal!" screamed Miss Regina, slashing out for about the fifth time and missing again. Beside herself with rage, she suddenly rode her horse straight at it, trying to trample it to death. The children screamed with terror. But the cat leapt like a tiger up towards the rider, failed to reach her, and for a moment, hissing and wild-eyed, it hung from the horse's neck. The horse let out a shrill neigh and reared up on its hind legs. Anna rushed forward and snatched the baby out of the way of the horse's hooves. Miss Regina thrashed round with her crop, the children screamed, the cat scratched and spat, and the next moment the horse bolted wildly down the hill. Miss Regina was a skilful horsewoman, so remained in the saddle, but the cat soon let go and fell to the ground. It landed on its feet and apparently unhurt, its fur standing on end, it fled into the forest.

Ida came peering sleepily out on to the porch, woken from her afternoon nap on the kitchen sofa by the noise. She shaded her eyes with her hand.

"What's going on?" she called. "What're you all up to, now?" She did not wait for an answer, but just went on in the same breath: "Hurry up now with them sticks, so I can get the fire going for coffee."

Anna put the baby down and John scrambled out from under the sawing-horse where he had fallen in terror. They looked at each other and then at the weeping children. John's voice trembled as he spoke.

"Oh, heavens, Anna . . . who was that? That person with such evil eyes?"

Anna looked down the hill where the rider had vanished, and her voice also trembled.

"That was Miss Regina, from the manor," she said.

Still shaken, John went on:

"I was so frightened, Anna. She seemed wicked to me . . . it shone out of her eyes!"

"She didn't like the cat," said Anna. "We must tell Dally-Peter to keep his cat at home. Otherwise they might shoot the poor thing."

"Yes," said John, hurriedly picking up an armful of sticks, as Ida was shouting from the porch again.

"What're you doing, there? Come on! Can't you hear me. I want my coffee, you brats."

That week there were no gifts from the manor and Karlberg muttered crossly because there was neither any coffee nor butter left.

"They've forgotten, I expect, now the landlord's away," he said. "Nothing's done proper down there no longer."

"How can I get by without my Sunday cup of coffee," moaned Ida, going out on to the porch again and again and looking down the hill, but the evening went by and no trap came.

"You'll have to tell them tomorrow," Karlberg said to Anna. "Go on down to the manor tomorrow, and tell them to bring up what's due to us."

So Anna went down to the manor the next day and was met by a very nervous and upset Mademoiselle.

"Oh, oh!" she wailed. "Just imagine what's happened! Mr Sylvester's ill faraway in a foreign country and can't come back. He should know he's too old to go on such long and difficult journeys. You can't rush round the world like that when you're old. You should stay where you belong then. Oh, dear, what a thing, what a thing! The worry of it gets you down. And such a terrible illness, too . . . *typhoid fever*! No, child, you wouldn't know, but it's a very dangerous disease, very dangerous . . . perhaps Mr Sylvester will never come back again."

"What are you saying, Mademoiselle!" whispered Anna. "Is he so ill? So ill he might die?"

"Yes, yes," wailed Mademoiselle, rocking back and forth. "It bodes ill, it does, an old man like him, and such a dreadful disease. No, no, it bodes ill, it does."

"But . . ." said Anna. "We can't leave him there in that foreign country, lying there ill and alone."

"Oh," said Mademoiselle. "And who can go all the way down there to fetch him back? You, perhaps? Or me, an old body like me? Or one of the maids? Or a labourer? No, indeed, that would be no good, either. *We* can do nothing for Mr Sylvester. But one would expect Miss Regina would perhaps think . . ."

"Think *what*, Mademoiselle?" Miss Regina was suddenly standing in the doorway, in riding habit as usual, her crop in her hand. "Wouldn't it be better if Mademoiselle kept her thoughts to herself," she said, her voice sharp and cutting. "A crofter's brat is hardly the most suitable confessor, is it? Anyhow, you should know better than most, Mademoiselle, after all these years, that servants should not discuss their employers."

Two red patches appeared on Mademoiselle's cheeks, but she said nothing, as the correction had been justified. Miss Regina was right and Mademoiselle wrong. But it was hard on an old person like Mademoiselle to be reprimanded by someone young enough to be her granddaughter.

Miss Regina turned to Anna and touched her with her riding crop.

"Come with me," she said.

She took Anna out on to the veranda with her, out of earshot of Mademoiselle and the maids.

"You know that I give orders here now, don't you?" she said. "You have just heard that my Uncle is ill and will perhaps never come back."

"Yes," said Anna.

"Then you should hear what I have to say. I do not wish to see you here any more. I *never* want to see you here again. Have you understood?"

"Yes," said Anna, understanding nothing. Wasn't she to be allowed down at the manor again? Never again sit in that nice kitchen, eating good cakes, Mademoiselle's friendly hand stroking her head? Never again see Mr Sylvester? Never again see the picture of Annemaria Beatrice Frederika? *Never again?*

She gazed at Miss Regina, as if waiting for further explanation, or at least some change in expression that might soften the harshness of her words and say that she had meant no ill.

But Miss Regina's eyes were dark and icy cold, and Anna froze beneath her gaze.

"She doesn't like me," ran through her mind. "She doesn't like me."

Confused and miserable, she turned away and walked down the veranda steps, across the front gravel, where the fountain was playing, the flower-beds resplendent round it. But before she closed the great iron gates behind her, she turned round and looked back up at the manor house, and there was Miss Regina, still standing on the veranda steps. Straight and slim in her black riding habit, the crop in her hand, she seemed to Anna like the angel with the burning sword, guarding the entrance to the Garden of Eden.

Back at Kulla, Ida was grumbling about the lack of coffee and neither Karlberg nor the children thought it advisable to stay indoors. Karlberg was sitting on a log down by the wood-pile, sunning himself, and the children were hanging about in a bunch by the stile, waiting for Anna to come back.

"Hi, hi, hi!" the baby sang out, waving happily when she caught sight of Anna's blue spotted dress down the hill. She knew that Anna was coming from the manor house, and thought that as usual there would be some extra titbit in her skirt pocket.

But today Anna did not wave back and looked so different, walking slowly with her head down, that the children were dismayed, aware that something was wrong. John ran down to meet her.

"Anna . . . what's the matter? What is it, Anna? Anna, you're not *crying*, are you?"

He stopped and stared in horror. "Are you *crying*, Anna?" he said again, unable to believe his eyes. He couldn't remember ever seeing Anna crying before.

Anna raised her eyes, her eyelashes full of tears.

"They say the landlord's going to die," she whispered. "And she . . . Miss Regina . . . doesn't want to see me down there again. I can never go down there again, never again, John."

John took her hand and patted it clumsily.

"Don't be miserable," he said, trying to comfort her. "You belong here with us, anyhow, Anna."

But Anna walked silently on and set about her chores. In the evening, when the milking and her jobs were done, she climbed up into the empty hay-loft and stood looking out through the opening down at the manor. The long avenue of aspen trees lay like a green garland along the line of the river and at the end of it, the great white building sat like a shining jewel in the summer evening mist. Anna thought about everything she had experienced down there, and about Mr Sylvester who would probably never return. He had been so kind to her and perhaps, perhaps if they had belonged together . . . grandfather and granddaughter, oh, perhaps if it had been so . . . She could not get it out of her thoughts, just as she could not stop thinking about the girl in the portrait, her names and so like herself . . . well, she knew that an understanding existed between them.

Anna leant her forehead against the rough wood of the wall and the evening wind streaming through the opening stirred her fair curls. Her heart ached with longing.

"Annemaria Beatrice Frederika," she thought. "Will I never be allowed to see you again?"